D1438974

AMERICAN HERITAGE

October 1963 · Volume XIV, Number 6

ADDISON GALLERY OF AMERICAN ART, PHILLIPS ACADEMY, ANDOVER, MASS.

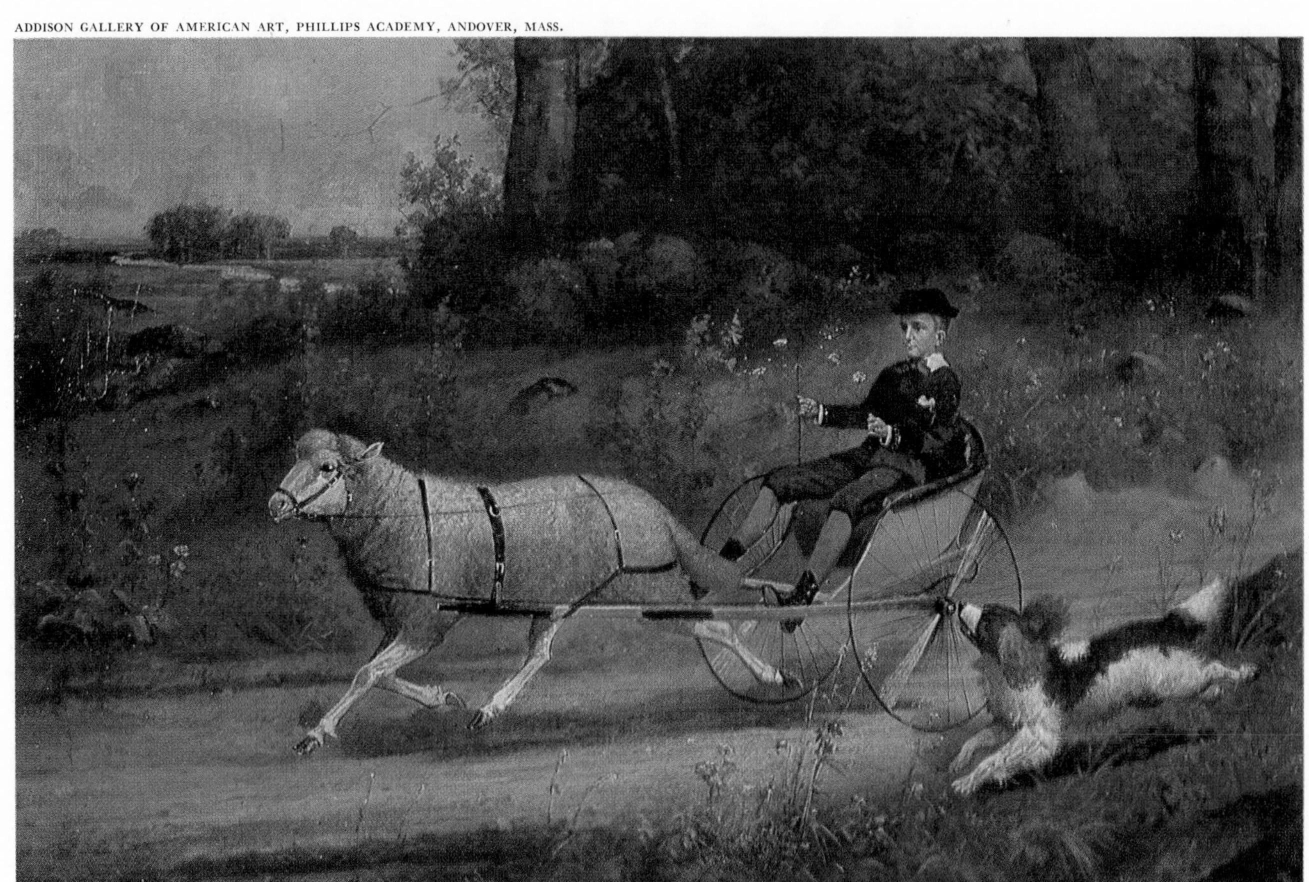

This strange painting, titled The Young Aristocrat, *almost defies comment. If the expression of the boy in the Fauntleroy costume is apprehensive—and even (one hesitates to say it) sheepish—who can wonder? Is he to the manor borne? The artist responsible for this somewhat jaded pastoral of the Gilded Age is one Nicholas Winfield Scott Leighton of Boston, a man who was apparently most noted for his sensitive and refined portraits of horses. It is recorded that when he became aware that his hackneys were becoming hackneyed, he commenced the serious study of cattle, fowl, and other domestic animals. He died in an insane asylum.*

AMERICAN HERITAGE

The Magazine of History

AMERICAN HERITAGE is published every two months by American Heritage Publishing Co., Inc., 551 Fifth Avenue, New York 17, N.Y. Correspondence about subscriptions should be addressed to: American Heritage Subscription Office, 383 West Center Street, Marion, Ohio. Single Copies: $3.95. Annual Subscriptions: $15.00 in U.S. & Canada; $16.00 elsewhere.

An annual Index of AMERICAN HERITAGE is published every February, priced at $1.00. A Cumulative Index of Volumes VI–X is available at $3.00.

Second class postage paid at New York, N.Y., and at additional mailing offices.

Sponsored by
American Association for State & Local History · Society of American Historians

CONTENTS *October 1963 · Volume XIV, Number 6*

COVER: Around the bend comes the monster—a wood-burning engine of the 1850's—belching cinders and smoke and fire. At the neigh of the iron horse, the flesh-and-blood variety darts off across the landscape, eyes wide in fright, tail and mane flying. The moral seems plain indeed: like frontier America itself, the untamed ways of this carefree creature must inevitably succumb to the onrush of civilization. An artist named A. Tapy did this fine primitive in 1859; it comes from the notable American art collection of Edgar William and Bernice Chrysler Garbisch. *Back Cover:* The *Chancellor Livingston* was the last steamer to be designed by Robert Fulton, but he died before she was launched in 1816. This handsome ship operated on the New York-to-Albany run for years; later, completely rebuilt, she plied the waters off the New England coast. The lithograph by Moses Swett, reproduced through the courtesy of the Mariners Museum in Newport News, Virginia, shows her in the twilight of a career that ended in 1842. For the story of Fulton; his benefactor, Robert R. Livingston; and their great water-borne monopoly, see "The Steamboat's Charter of Freedom," beginning on page 38.

Nature's God

From his pulpit in Christ Episcopal Church in Philadelphia, Dr. James Abercrombie looked out at a congregation that included the first President of the United States. He had good reason to feel some nervousness on this particular Sunday morning, for he was about to perform an act of ecclesiastical daring. He was about to scold George Washington, in public, for his religious behavior.

Dr. Abercrombie mentioned no names as he pitched into a sermon on the grave responsibility of "those in elevated stations" to set good examples for lesser folk, but only the children in his pews that day could have missed the point. He focussed on the celebration of the Lord's Supper; and everyone knew that President Washington habitually joined those who walked out of church, on communion Sundays, just before the sacrament was to be administered. The rector's target was embarrassingly clear.

No doubt Dr. Abercrombie hoped to achieve the pious triumph of persuading the President to take holy communion at his altar. But, although his message had not passed the presidential ears unheeded, the outcome was disconcerting. Washington never again left the church just before the Lord's Supper—from that time forward he did not come at all on communion Sundays.

The minister swallowed his disappointment as best he could. Writing, years later, to someone who had inquired about Washington's religion, he said that according to one of the President's acquaintances—he could not remember precisely whom—the great man preferred to stay away rather than become a communicant because, "were he to become one then, it would be imputed to an ostentatious display of religious zeal." This was a relatively consoling explanation, but there are signs that it failed to convince Dr. Abercrombie himself. "That Washington was a professing Christian," he added to his correspondent, "is evident from his regular attendance in our church, but sir, I cannot consider any man as a real Christian who uniformly disregards an ordinance so solemnly enjoined by the divine Author of our holy religion. . . ."

What were Washington's reasons for refusing to partake in the Lord's Supper? Exact answers are lost to history, concealed behind the reticence he steadily maintained where his private beliefs were concerned. In terms of reasonable inference, however, it is possible to offer an explanation. He had long been exposed to the ideas of the European Enlightenment, and his behavior suggests that his religious views were considerably shaped thereby. It was an intellectual atmosphere not favorable to symbolic rites, among other things. In his exposure to it, Washington was of course far from unique among the Founding Fathers of the American republic. Inevitably, all of his educated contemporaries were to some extent children of the Age of Reason (as Tom Paine called it); and among them several of the acknowledged political leaders were certainly its eminent sons.

Still, there was no great uniformity of opinion among the Founding Fathers on specific religious or philosophical questions. Whether one considers the signers of the Declaration of Independence or the delegates to the Constitutional Convention of 1787, or both, it is easy to find a diversity of sects and creeds. But the broad spectrum of denominations is itself a reminder that a prime characteristic of the Enlightenment was respect for dissenting opinions. The famous remark attributed to Voltaire, "I may disagree with what you say, but I will defend to the death your

Jefferson and Madison led a revolutionary fight for complete separation of church and state. Their reasons probed the basic relation between religion and democracy

...nd the Founding Fathers

By E. M. HALLIDAY

right to say it," catches the spirit of the era. While full freedom of belief was not legally protected in any of the colonies at the start of the Revolution, and most of them had an established church supported by the government, minority groups and nonconforming individuals were in fact granted considerable leeway. Catholics were strong in Maryland; Quakers, in Pennsylvania. In New England, the evolution of Congregational doctrine had moved toward freedom of conscience for more than a century, so that there was a kind of paradox in the legal establishment of a church so nearly democratic in its organization. The supremacy of the Anglicans in the South, moreover, was weakened by the fact that theirs was the official church of England in a period when independence from the mother country was about to become the paramount fact of current history. For, whatever their doctrinal differences in religion, all of the Founding Fathers were political revolutionaries, determined to enact a new formulation of the idea of government by consent of the governed.

Even Washington's most ardent admirers have never claimed that he was, philosophically, a deep thinker. Thomas Jefferson, by contrast, was as philosophically inclined, and gifted with as keen an analytical mind, as any American of his time. His interest in religion and its proper relationship to government was intense, and it persisted throughout his long life. During his second term as President (1805–1809) he sought relief from the tremendous pressures of his office by composing, for his own satisfaction, a version of the New Testament which he called "The Life and Morals of Jesus of Nazareth." It would have interested Washington, for among many other significant omissions it pointedly left out the story of the Last Supper. This was as good a clue as any to Jefferson's idea in undertaking the work, which was, in his own sharp language, to rescue from "the speculations of crazy theologists" the moral teachings of Jesus, "abstracting what is really his from the rubbish in which it is buried."

In his own terms, Jefferson claimed to be a Christian—but he assuredly was not one according to Dr. Abercrombie's standards, or for that matter according to the doctrine of any organized Christian church, unless it was the fledgling Unitarian. He rejected, he wrote, "the immaculate conception of Jesus, his deification, the creation of the world by him, his miraculous powers, his resurrection and visible ascension, his corporeal presence in the Eucharist, the Trinity, original sin, atonement, regeneration, election, orders of Hierarchy, etc." He thought of Christ as a great reformer, author of "a system of the most sublime morality which has ever fallen from the lips of man"—but human rather than divine. To be a Christian, for Jefferson, was simply to follow the system of ethics taught by Christ, uncontaminated by what he considered the additions, adulterations, and distortions of those who came after. And Jefferson thought he had an easy touchstone for distinguishing Jesus' original teachings from the dross. All that was needed was the "free exercise of reason": with that, the genu-

NEW JERSEY STATE HISTORICAL SOCIETY

ine precepts of the Master would never be found to disagree.

To orthodox clergymen and theologians this was heresy; it was, many of them angrily charged, a mere disguise for atheism. As a prominent political figure, Jefferson often suffered from his refusal to accept traditional Christianity, even though he tried to keep his religious views largely to himself. His skepticism toward anything alleged to be supernatural was misunderstood, and his high regard for Christian ethics was usually ignored. Shocking stories circulated long before he became a presidential candidate, and their currency grew with his fame. John Trumbull, the great painter of the Revolution, told one about a dinner party at Jefferson's home in 1793, when the future President sat "smiling and nodding approbation" while Congressman William Giles of Virginia—a fellow skeptic—"proceeded so far . . . as to ridicule the character, conduct and doctrines of the divine founder of our religion." This was unquestionably an exaggeration, but it suggests Jefferson's reputation at the time. When he was presidential runner-up in 1796, a minister in Connecticut took note of the event in a prayer before his congregation: "O Lord! wilt Thou bestow upon the Vice President a double portion of Thy grace, *for Thou knowest he needs it.*" In the campaign of 1800 Jefferson's "infidelity" was an easy target for Federalist orators and pamphleteers.

Yet there is little doubt that Jefferson held a profound belief in a Supreme Being. In a fashion typical of eighteenth-century intellectuals, he held it not on implicit faith, but as a reasoned conclusion based on evidence and deduction. "I hold (without appeal to revelation)," he once wrote to John Adams, "that when we take a view of the universe, in its parts, general or particular, it is impossible for the human mind not to perceive and feel a conviction of design, consummate skill, and indefinite power in every atom of its composition." Newton and his contemporaries in the seventeenth century had magnificently demonstrated that man lived in a universe of precise mathematical law and order; it seemed scientifically evident to most thinkers in the following era that such a cosmic design could come only from the hand of a divine Creator.

It was a long way from the theology of traditional Christianity, this idea of an invisible but demonstrable God whose existence was proved only by His handiwork; for "He" was now a nearly impersonal power, responsible for the origin and laws of the universe, but not interfering in its operation once the myriad wheels of the great machine had been set in motion. This was "Nature's God," as Jefferson phrased it in the Declaration of Independence; and to him and many others the religion appropriate to Nature's God must be natural, not supernatural, in its foundations. Deism, or "natural religion," expressed their theological creed, not a Christianity based on revelation, mystery, and miracle.

Some men—notably a prominent group in France including Diderot, d'Alembert, Condorcet, and the Baron d'Holbach—went further, postulating an automatic universe, operating by inexorable natural laws, but utterly devoid of God or God's purpose. Jefferson was inclined to resist this surge toward atheism, yet it is only justice to the true character of his mind to emphasize that his attitude was far from fanatical. He was never an absolutist, even on the question of God's existence. His creed of intellectual freedom was much too firm for that, and at worst he saw no alarming threat in atheism. Before he went to France to be United States minister from 1784 to 1789, he had already considered the effects of full disbelief. "It does me no injury for my neighbor to say there are twenty Gods, or no God," he observed in his *Notes on Virginia* (1782). "It neither picks my pocket nor breaks my leg." And writing to his young nephew, Peter Carr, from Paris in 1787, he urged him to make reason his guide: ". . . call to her tribunal every fact, every opinion. Question with boldness even the existence of a God; because, if there be one, he must more approve of the homage of reason, than that of blindfolded fear."

Jefferson's vital disposition toward freedom of thought was strengthened by his five years in France. Not only was he there a first-hand observer of the moral and material degradation resulting, as he saw it, from the combination of religious persecution and tyrannical government. In that cosmopolitan air he also made familiar contact with many of the most brilliant figures of the age. The political, philosophical, and religious ideas of the Enlightenment now reached him not just in books, but in absorbing conversations across his own dinner table. Voltaire had written that atheists, deplorable as they might be, would still make better neighbors than religious fanatics. Jefferson came to know some of the leading French atheists as friends and acquaintances, and he found them anything but monsters. "Diderot, D'Alembert, D'Holbach, Condorcet," he wrote to a friend years later, "are known to have been among the most virtuous of men. Their virtue, then, must have had some other foundation than the love of God."

This crucial question of the basis of human morality, bearing as it does on the relation between religion and government, intrigued Jefferson all his life. He early formed an opinion consistent with the natural religion of the Enlightenment, and from it he never

METROPOLITAN MUSEUM OF ART, GIFT OF MRS. A. WORDSWORTH THOMPSON, 1899

The unruffled atmosphere of an Anglican Sunday in colonial Virginia is suggested in Alfred Wordsworth Thompson's nineteenth-century painting of Bruton Parish Church in Williamsburg, a building still in use. Here planters gathered as much to conduct business as to worship. As one contemporary observer commented, "it is not the custom for Gentlemen to go into Church til Service is beginning, when they enter in a Body, in the same manner as they come out; I have known the Clerk to come . . . call them in to prayers."

swerved throughout the remainder of his eighty-three years. Its essence was natural morality. "Man was destined for society," he wrote to his nephew in 1787. ". . . He was endowed with a sense of right and wrong, merely relative to this. This sense is as much a part of his nature, as the sense of hearing, seeing, feeling; it is the true foundation of morality. . . . The moral sense, or conscience, is as much a part of man as his leg or arm." And while Jefferson firmly believed that this moral sense was the gift of a divine Creator, he was equally certain that acknowledgment of its source was not necessary to its function. If young Peter Carr, having fully considered the evidence, were to become an atheist, still, Jefferson assured him, "you will find incitements to virtue in the comfort and pleasantness you feel in its exercise, and the love of others which it will procure you."

Jefferson's theory of natural morality was for him the cornerstone of the democratic faith which he did so much during his lifetime to make a living reality. The church doctrine of original sin was anathema to him. Human nature could be trusted: all normal men were endowed by their Creator not only with unalienable rights, but with unalienable instincts, including a natural moral sense. Except under bad social conditions—ignorance, poor education, poverty—the mass of men, he felt, would surely gravitate toward what was right on fundamental issues, if only they were allowed complete freedom of conscience. The principle of majority rule—a sacred principle to Jefferson—depended on the premise of a well-informed public, each member of which could choose among moral or political alternatives with absolute freedom from mental coercion.

This is the key to Jefferson's lifelong insistence on complete separation of church and state. While it was a matter of democratic principle with him to champion full freedom of voluntary association, so that any number of divergent sects could thrive without government interference, he had no sympathy for their dogmatic approach to questions of moral truth. An organized church, he thought, was unlikely to leave men's minds completely free. Whatever the denomination, each claimed a special revelation of God's will, imparted directly to its prophets or priests, or recorded in the Bible. (Franklin, whose views were much like Jefferson's, said that religious sects reminded him of "a certain French lady who, in a dispute with her sister, said, 'I don't know how it happens, sister, but I meet with nobody but myself that's always in the right!' ") Few were therefore willing to relinquish moral (and, by implication, political) choices to the untrammelled conscience of the individual citizen.

Jefferson had the good fortune to live long and to compose his own epitaph after much deliberation. It was a modest statement for a man who had been among the foremost in establishing the American na-

CONTINUED ON PAGE 100

THE Tragic Dream OF Jean Ribaut

Half a century before Jamestown, a Huguenot sea captain planted the flag of France on America's South Atlantic coast. His hopes were as high as the odds against him

By SHERWOOD HARRIS

By the year 1561 the mainland of North America had acquired a bad reputation, at least as far as Spain was concerned. In the three-score years following Columbus' electrifying voyage, several Spanish attempts to colonize the Gulf and Atlantic coasts had failed dismally. Ponce de Léon was dead from wounds suffered during an Indian attack in Florida. The ambitious De Soto now lay at rest beneath the wide waters of the Mississippi which he had discovered. Pánfilo de Narváez had disappeared in the Gulf of Mexico, the only survivors among his six hundred men being a handful of gaunt and naked wanderers who miraculously made their way to safety in Mexico (see "The Ordeal of Cabeza de Vaca" in the December, 1960, AMERICAN HERITAGE). Despite its early promise, this vast new country had produced no Eldorado, no Fountain of Youth, no short cut to the riches of the Orient. It was, in brief, far less attractive in every respect than Mexico and Peru.

And so on September 23, 1561, King Philip II of Spain declared the mainland off limits to further official Spanish efforts. It was almost inevitable that Philip's decision would prove to be a tactical mistake. Though Spain was at peace with France at the moment, French pirates operating in the Florida straits were taking an alarming toll of the heavily laden treasure galleons bound for Spain. And Philip's ambassador in Paris warned that plans were afoot to plant a military outpost in Florida. But Philip apparently felt secure in the belief that if mighty Spain could not make a colony stick, France, beset by internal religious and political disorders, was hardly in a position to do better.

Had Philip known about, or been in a position to gauge the character of the man who was about to prove him wrong, he might have reacted differently. This man was Jean Ribaut, a bold French Huguenot sea captain in his early forties who had powerful friends in France and at the court of Queen Elizabeth in England. Ribaut was a man of deeds, rather than words; his only extant writings are contained in a short report of his first trip to the New World. But wherever he went, whatever he did, he moved men and caused things to happen. Thus four hundred years

Ribaut first sighted land on April 30, 1562, at Cape François (Promontorium Gallicum, *left*)*, somewhere near modern St. Augustine, Florida. When this first landfall revealed no harbor, he continued north until he came upon a sizable stream which he called the River of May—known today as the St. Johns. There, in the scene depicted above, he was welcomed and feted by friendly Indians. (The artist, however, seems to have confused the River of May with another landmark not far to the south, the River of Dolphins* [F(luvium) Delfinum] *—most probably St. Augustine Inlet, a poor harbor, which Ribaut missed.) This and the engravings on the next six pages are by Theodore de Bry, and were first published at Frankfort in 1591. They are based on the work of Jacques le Moyne de Morgues, who accompanied Ribaut's lieutenant, René de Laudonnière, on the second French expedition to Florida in 1564. Le Moyne did some forty-two paintings which De Bry later acquired. Only one of them (see page 13) still exists.*

afterward we can get a clear impression of this remarkable adventurer and the events he set in motion.

On February 16, 1562, true to the Spanish ambassador's warning, Ribaut set out from Le Havre with two ships, a large sloop, and a company of some 150 sailors, harquebusiers, and adventurous young French Protestant noblemen and officers. This was, in effect, an expeditionary force sent out "to discover and view a certaine long coast of the West India," as Ribaut wrote in his single surviving manuscript, quoted here from the sixteenth-century translation printed in Hakluyt's *Divers Voyages.* If all went well, farmers and artisans and supplies would be sent later, thus establishing a permanent refuge in the New World for France's harried Huguenots. A successful colony would also act as a safety valve in relieving Huguenot political pressure on France's Catholic government, pressure strong enough at that moment to threaten civil war.

At daybreak on the morning of April 30, seventy-three days out from Le Havre, Ribaut's lookouts spotted a long, low, palm-fringed promontory some-

*Leaving the River of May, Ribaut explored along the Atlantic coast and on May 17 put into a harbor he called Port Royal (*Portus Regalis, *at left) in present-day South Carolina. Here his men built Charlesfort, near the present Marine "boot camp" on Parris Island. Ribaut returned to France for more colonists and supplies, leaving a volunteer garrison behind. These men (right) raised no food and soon "found themselves in such extremity" that they were forced to appeal to friendly Indians "to succour them in their necessity." Finally giving up hope of ever seeing Ribaut again (he had first become involved in the Catholic-Huguenot wars, and later found himself in an English jail), they built a small boat and set out for home. After travelling more than 3,000 horror-filled miles, they were rescued at sea and taken to Le Havre, fed up with the New World.*

where in the vicinity of present-day St. Augustine, Florida. Ribaut anchored and lowered his pinnaces to explore. The small boats returned shortly after noon with the news that they had found no harbor for the ships. Ribaut weighed anchor and headed north, naming his first landfall in the New World Cape François, in honor of his native land.

Toward evening on the first day, still heading north along the coast with "unspeakable pleasure," Ribaut perceived "a leaping and a breaking of the water, as a streame falling out of the lande into the Sea." He anchored and spent the night there, restlessly awaiting the dawn so he could go ashore and explore what was apparently the mouth of a large fresh-water river.

"The next day, in the morning, being the first of May, wee assayed to enter this Porte," Ribaut continued. Apparently the curious Indians who came to see what was going on had as yet suffered no misfortunes at the hands of white men, though Spanish ships had visited the east coast of Florida before. The Indians showed Ribaut the best places to beach his boats and welcomed him by exchanging gifts. The women and children, shy at first, soon gathered in great numbers, bringing with them evergreen boughs which they spread out on the sand for their chief and his visitors to relax upon while they tried to communicate.

In keeping with the month and the mood of his reception, Ribaut named his discovery the River of May. (We know it today as the St. Johns, that fascinating stream that flows north from Florida's lake country, past the seaport of Jacksonville, and on out to the ocean past the aircraft carrier docks at Mayport.) Ribaut spent two days exploring the mouth of the May and in planting one of two stone columns he had brought with him to stake out France's claim to this part of the New World. Replenishing the ships' supplies was no problem; the Indians on the north shore soon began competing with a different tribe on the south bank to see which could outdo the other in hospitality. They plied Ribaut and his men with fresh fish, oysters, crabs, lobsters, beans, meal cakes, fresh water—Ribaut's account at this point reads much like that of a man who was pretty well fed up with two and a half months of shipboard fare.

BOTH, LIBRARY OF CONGRESS

Lured on by vague Spanish reports of a mighty "River Jordan" farther north, Ribaut left the May and pushed on up the coast past the sounds and rivers of Georgia. These he extravagantly named after the great waterways of France: the Seine, the Somme, the Loire, and so on.

As the expedition passed the present Georgia-South Carolina border around the middle of May, "great fogges and tempests" overtook them. The two ships were forced to head for the safety of deep water. The pinnaces, working in closer to shore, lost contact with their mother ships, but when the storm cleared a day later, they raced out to join forces again, excitedly reporting that they had ridden out the gale in a harbor bigger and more beautiful than any encountered so far.

Ribaut crossed the bar of this new discovery on May 17, 1562. Describing it as "one of the fayrest and greatest Havens of the worlde," Ribaut named the harbor Port Royal. One of his lieutenants, a young nobleman named René de Laudonnière, echoed the awe of the French seamen as they sailed into the magnificent bay: "the depth is such . . . that the greatest shippes of France, yea, the Arguzes of Venice may enter in there."

Ribaut's soldiers and sailors were not the first white men to visit Port Royal. As near as we can tell from conflicting accounts of his voyage, Lucas Vázquez de Ayllón of Santo Domingo had come this way with a Spanish expedition in the 1520's. In honor of the saint's day on which the harbor was discovered, he had christened it St. Helena, a name that still survives among the Sea Islands of the South Carolina coast. And a year before Ribaut's arrival, a Spanish expedition under Angel de Villafañe had explored the area under orders from King Philip II to find a suitable place for a permanent colony. But Villafañe turned in such a negative report that his voyage served only to hasten Philip's decision to forget about the mainland.

After exploring the broad reaches of the Port Royal harbor and its tributaries, Ribaut concluded that the country was even fairer than that surrounding the River of May. "Wee founde the Indians there more doubtfull and fearefull then the others before," he wrote. "Yet after we had been in their houses and con-

LIBRARY OF CONGRESS

With Ribaut languishing in prison, Laudonnière arrived at the River of May in 1564. The Indians received him hospitably, and the chief's son, Athore, showed Laudonnière a pillar Ribaut had previously erected. "On approaching," Le Moyne wrote, "[the French] found that these Indians were worshipping this stone as an idol." In the single surviving Le Moyne painting, this scene is depicted at right. Back at the mouth of the May, Laudonnière laid out a site for a new defense point (left), which he called Fort Caroline. The next day, Le Moyne reported, "after offering prayers to God and giving thanks for their prosperous arrival, they all went briskly to work . . . some to dig the earth, some to make brushwood fascines, some to put up a wall. Every man was engaged with spade, saw, axe, or other tool; and so diligent were they that the work went rapidly . . ."

gregated with them, and shewed curtesie . . . they were somewhat emboldened." Ribaut planted his second stone column and summoned his men to his flagship to discuss their next move.

"I thinke there is none of you that is ignorant of how great consequence this our enterprize is, and also how acceptable it is unto our yong King," he began. Reiterating the point that all who heeded him would be highly commended to the French court, Ribaut then asked for volunteers to stay in Port Royal while he returned to France for reinforcements. "You shalbe registred for ever as the first that inhabited this strang[e] countrey," he concluded.

Ribaut was apparently overwhelmed with volunteers. He picked roughly two dozen soldiers to remain behind and retained all his sailors for the return voyage to France. At the request of the men who were to stay on, Ribaut built a fort which he named Charlesfort in honor of his sovereign, Charles IX. Ribaut stocked it with food and left cannon, harquebuses, and ammunition with the soldiers. On June 11 the two ships departed, Ribaut indulging a bit in his favorite sport of river exploring before heading east for France. He promised to return in six months with more colonists and supplies.

At this point Ribaut concludes his account of the first French settlement in America. He was fated never to see his tiny colony again. For when he reached France the political tides had turned against the Huguenots. Civil war had broken out, embroiling the Protestant citizens of Ribaut's native Dieppe in a series of battles with the Catholic forces of the government. Ribaut fought alongside his townsmen, and when the city capitulated in October of 1562 he fled to England.

There he tried to interest Queen Elizabeth in supporting his colony. An expedition was arranged under the notorious entrepreneur Thomas Stukely, but Ribaut became suspicious of his motives. Fearing that Stukely might force the colony to swear allegiance to England, Ribaut secretly decided to back out of the deal and make off to France with some of the ships that had been readied for the

PRINT ROOM, NEW YORK PUBLIC LIBRARY

voyage. The plot was discovered. Seized before he could make good his escape, Ribaut was thrown into prison for two years.

The colony at Port Royal prospered at first. The site Ribaut had chosen could hardly have been better. Temperate in climate and healthy, the country surrounding Port Royal abounded in wildlife of staggering variety. Even today a few minutes' walk across the tidal flats at any time of the year will produce a meal of oysters and clams; the woods are full of deer, wild turkeys, and other game. As Ribaut noted in his report, "there is so many small byrdes, that it is a strange thing to bee seene." Port Royal, in short, was "one of the goodliest, best, and fruitefullest countreys that ever was seene."

Having no knowledge of the events that were to prevent their commander from returning on schedule, however, the men at Charlesfort made no provision to live off the land. Fortunately, they were on good terms with the local Indians. Continuing with the story of the Port Royal settlement from the point where Ribaut leaves off, René de Laudonnière writes: "their victualles beganne to waxe short, which forced them to have recourse unto their neighbors . . . which gave them part of all the victualles which they had, and kept no more unto themselves [than] would serve to sow their fieldes."

As the fall of 1562 wore on without sight of a sail, the stores of the nearby Indian tribes began to run low because of the additional burdens placed on them by the colonists. The natives retired deeper into the woods to forage on roots and nuts and whatever game they could kill. At this point a disastrous fire broke out at Charlesfort, consuming almost all the Frenchmen's remaining supplies. For a time they were able to sustain themselves by trading knives and trinkets with more distant tribes, "but misfortune or rather the just judgment of God would have it," wrote Laudonnière, "that those which could not bee overcome by fire nor water, should be undone by their owne selves."

When Ribaut departed for France he had placed the garrison under the command of Captain Albert de la Pierria, a soldier of long experience who seems to have

Like their predecessors at Charlesfort, the French at Fort Caroline depended for their food supply on the Indians, whose agricultural methods Le Moyne portrayed at left. "When the ground is sufficiently broken up and levelled," he wrote, "the women come with beans and millet, or maize. Some go first with a stick and make holes, in which the others place the beans, or grains." They then sought shelter in the forest for the winter, harvesting late in the spring. Eventually the Indians rebelled against the French demands, however, and under a chief named Holata Outina (right) attacked Laudonnière's men. Outina "used to march with regular ranks . . . himself walking alone in the middle of the whole force, painted red." It was a grim portent of the Spanish attack which in September, 1565, destroyed Fort Caroline, dashing the brave hopes of Jean Ribault.

been something of a martinet. As the problems of survival in the New World became more urgent, the Captain dealt more and more severely with his men. He hanged a drummer named Guernache for a "smal fault"; then, because of some unrecorded misdemeanor, he banished a soldier named La Chère to a tiny uninhabited island nearby. Though the Captain promised La Chère food and water, he failed to keep his word. The other soldiers mutinied, killed the Captain, and rescued the starving La Chère. Returning to Charlesfort, they resolved to build a boat in which to return to France. The six months were up, and Ribaut had not returned.

In all the annals of the sea there is nothing quite like the voyage of this handful of French soldiers back to their native land. Though Ribaut's men probably did not realize it, the distance from Port Royal to Le Havre is approximately 3,500 miles.* Ribaut had taken all his sailors back with him to France. Thus the Charlesfort garrison had no real idea of the magnitude of the voyage they were about to attempt. Nor did they really know much about building a boat. With the aid of friendly Indians, no doubt happy to learn that they were about to get rid of the insatiable soldiers, Ribaut's men nevertheless put together a vessel they deemed seaworthy. Its seams were caulked with pine resin and Spanish moss; its sails were patched together from shirts and sheets. Not surprisingly, one of the party, a youth named Guillaume Rouffi, elected to remain at Charlesfort rather than take his chances on the open sea in so crude a boat.

René de Laudonnière, who interviewed the survivors of this remarkable voyage, estimated that the soldiers were well along their way across the wintry Atlantic when they had their first setback. "After they had sayled the third part of their way, they were surprized with calmes which did so much hinder them, that in three weekes they sailed not above five and twentie leagues," he wrote. They rationed their remaining food, each receiving twelve grains of mill a day.

* In 1789 Captain William Bligh covered 3,618 miles in an open boat in forty-three days following the famous mutiny aboard *H.M.S. Bounty*, but Bligh had a sturdy boat and an unusually capable and well-disciplined crew.

BOTH, LIBRARY OF CONGRESS

"Yea, and this felicitie lasted not long," Laudonnière continued. "For their victuals failed them altogether at once: and they had nothing for their more assured refuge but their shooes and leather jerkins which they did eat . . . some of them dranke the sea water, others did drink their owne urine: and they remained in such desperate necessitie a very long space, during the which part of them died for hunger."

The calm that plagued them now gave way to a storm. "As men resolved to die," they settled down in the bilges to await the end. One man, however, still had his wits about him. He convinced his comrades that if the wind continued blowing from the same quadrant, they would sight land in three days. The storm abated, but by the end of three days no land had appeared.

"Wherefore in this extreme dispaire certaine among them made this motion that it was better that one man should dye, [than] that so many men should perish: they agreed therefore that one should die to sustaine the others," said Laudonnière. They drew lots and executed the loser. Ironically, this was La Chère, the soldier who had survived the unreasonable banishment. They divided La Chère's flesh among themselves —"a thing so pitiful to recite, that my pen is loth to write it," Laudonnière said.

Before it became necessary to resort to cannibalism a second time, land was sighted, and the survivors were picked up by an English barque. Among its crew was a Frenchman who had been on the first voyage to Port Royal, but who had returned to France with Ribaut. He recognized his emaciated compatriots and saw to it that they were well treated.

Throughout the rest of 1563 and on into early 1564, Guillaume Rouffi, the man who had mistrusted the crude boat, was France's sole representative on the mainland. In June, 1564, he was carted off to Havana by Don Hernando de Manrigue de Rojas, who had been sent out belatedly to get rid of the Charlesfort garrison.

Now the Atlantic Coast reverted to its native state. England had not yet put in a colonizing appearance. The failure of the Charlesfort colony had somewhat

CONTINUED ON PAGE 88

The COWHAND

Above: Erwin E. Smith about 1905, when he began to put the life of the range on film. Opposite: Smith set up his camera and tripod and had another cowhand snap this picture of him handling a rebellious mount on an Arizona ranch.

One of folklore's most romantic figures, the American cowboy, evolved, reached his zenith, and then nearly disappeared, all in little more than half a century. He left behind fewer authentic pictures of himself than the number of false images projected by television in a single week.

It is ironic that the most complete photographic record of the working cowboy was produced by a man who merely wanted to gather raw material until he could study art and become a sculptor of western life. In the meantime, Erwin E. Smith of Bonham, Texas, undertook to learn at first hand all there was to know about the things he wished to remember. "I knew that the life wouldn't wait; the technique would," he said. "So I put off Boston and the art schools as long as I could." Such was the genesis of the greatest collection of cowboy photographs ever made.

Smith brought to the task great natural gifts—tremendous patience, unsurpassed imagination, and a genius for composition and perspective. He came late to the scene, however. The long cattle drives to the north that began after the Civil War were over. The open-range grazing of the "beef bonanza" was steadily being transformed into ranching behind barbed-wire fences. Yet the equipment and work habits of the cowboy were still, briefly, what they had been in his heyday. Through Smith's pictures we are able to visualize the operations of the big outfits of the Southwest shortly before heavier breeds of beef, new marketing methods, and mechanical efficiencies changed the cowboy's life forever.

Smith's first experience on the range came in the summer of 1894, when, at the age of eight, he dogged the heels of his cousin Edwin Sanders on the JCS ranch near Quanah, Texas. During summer vacations, the boy was trained to the leather by cattlemen of the old school who ignored his youth and treated him like a regular cowhand.

Resolved to become an authority on the West and to capture the cowboy's life in art, Smith began experimenting with a box camera and developing fluids; while still in his teens he made several remarkably clear and well-composed pictures. In 1905 he set out for some of the bigger outfits of the Southwest. Would they hire him to work for small wages and permit him to take pictures of everyday ranch scenes? They would, and did; and for the better part of the next dozen summers he worked with the regular hands on many of the famous spreads in Texas, New Mexico, and Arizona.

For several winters Smith studied art in Chicago and in Boston; but somehow he never produced much sculpture. Instead, he himself became a Texas rancher—a financially unsuccessful one—for a number of years. But he never lost his obsession with producing a faithful photographic portrayal of the American cowboy, and before he died, in 1947, his collection of negatives had reached into the thousands. Some 1,800 of them are now in the Library of Congress, presented by Erwin Smith's sister, Mrs. L. M. Pettis. With her permission, AMERICAN HERITAGE reproduces on the following pages a representative group which shows the cowboy, in Smith's simple phrase, as "a man with work to do."

By ONA LEE McKEEN

BACON, BOOTS, AND SADDLES

The camp cook, almost invariably an old cowboy himself, was first up every morning to build the fire, boil the coffee, bake the sour-dough biscuits, and broil the bacon or steak for breakfast. He was unchallenged master of the chuck wagon, and though cowhands, like soldiers, might grumble about his food, they had no illusions about his rank and value. Smith's shot at left, made with the help of a little gunpowder tossed on the fire, shows the standard equipment. The rear end of the chuck wagon, opening out to form cupboards and work table, was a portable kitchen protected by a canvas fly. After breakfast there was the important business of choosing a mount from the outfit's remuda, *or horse herd (below). The best roper sometimes did the job for the others, flicking a lariat onto the desired horse as each rider called out his preference for the morning's work; others held a rope corral to keep the herd together. The typical western cow pony, even when thoroughly trained, was often "spooky," and not inclined to accept the saddle meekly. Smith captioned the sequence at right, taken on the Three-Circle Ranch in Texas, "The Usual Morning Fight." Actually, the whole procedure was likely to be repeated several times during the day when the outfit was on a drive or roundup: each cowboy required three or four daily mounts if the horses were not to be overworked.*

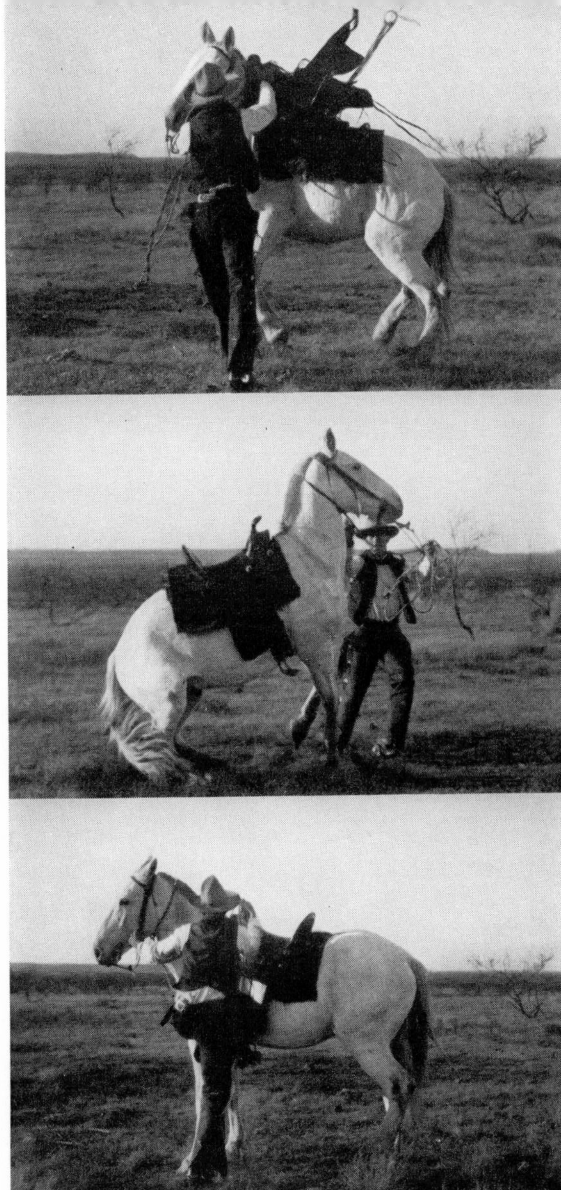

WATCHFUL

Spring and fall roundups were the big jobs in life on the western range. In between, the cattle were allowed to roam pretty much where their noses took them; but each spring the newly born calves had to be branded, and the whole herd had to be counted —a process involving much laborious search, rounding up, and separation of each rancher's cattle from those of his neighbors. In the fall, the chief object was to select those ready for shipment to the stockyards.

WORKING

During either roundup, someone had to watch the herd as it was gradually pulled together; and this—always exempting the chance of stampede—was the sort of quiet work depicted in Smith's placid composition shown above. At left, a range foreman diagrams in the dust the area each rider in his group will cover for the day; at right, the horse wrangler, remaining behind, pensively watches the remuda *until the cowpunchers come back in for a remount later in the day.*

TRICKS OF THE TRADE

The difficult feats now to be seen mostly in rodeos were still, in Erwin Smith's day, part of every cowhand's working life—the most strenuous and exacting part. Despite the coming of barbed wire, adjacent grazing lands were often not separated, and in any case there was much grazing on land leased in common, by several ranchers, from the government. Consequently there was a great mingling of stock, and at roundup time the herds had to be divided according to ownership. "Cutting out" a particular animal and maneuvering it into the right group without getting the rest of the herd too excited demanded a good rider on a superb horse—one specially trained for the job, with high intelligence, super-quick reflexes, and animal enthusiasm for the work. Above, two experts—man and mount—pivot sharply, anticipating the next move of the baffled cow. At left, an "outlaw" steer, who has gone semi-wild in his self-chosen isolation from the herd, is brought in by two ropers, while a third trails behind with his loop ready in case of trouble.

"Flanking" a roped calf for branding—that is, throwing it on the ground on its side—was a job that required strength, courage, nearly perfect timing, and a certain amount of luck. In the photo at right, Smith caught the action in the second before the calf hit the ground: the roper's horse holds steady, while the flanker's partner is poised to seize the animal's heels and pin him down. Below: A big calf is down and held, while a brander applies the hot iron that will make identification easy when fall roundup comes. As the iron sears in, the calf bawls like a hurt child—which indeed it is—and a gallery of apprehensive mothers sets up an antiphonal chorus in the background. If the calf is a male, and not selected (because of unusually fine quality) as a future breeding bull, further indignity follows immediately: a sharp knife in a practiced hand turns him into a young steer, and he is released to rejoin his mother—sadder, no wiser, but undeniably relieved. Roping, flanking, branding, and castrating was a team operation, and most cowboys developed specialties before they had been at the business very long.

SPECIAL ASSIGNMENT

At a big roundup, fairly distant ranches might each send a single cowhand—one with a good eye for reading brands—to cull out any stray cattle belonging to his employer. Here, such a "rep," travelling light with only two mounts and a bedroll, stops at a water hole for a drink from the brim of his hat.

HOME ON THE RANGE

Wherever the chuck wagon stopped for the night was home for the cowboy when he was working out on the range. Not only the source of all his "vittles," the wagon carried his bedroll, his drinking water, and what few first-aid supplies were available. The riders in the picture above are coming in for the evening meal with great spirit—no doubt partly for the benefit of Smith's camera. Left: An early supper for three cowhands who will probably go out as night herders when the rest of the crew comes in, to hold the cattle seen in the background. Some bedrolls are already spread out. Below: Tall tales around the fire were one of the cowboy's few diversions when the day's work was done.

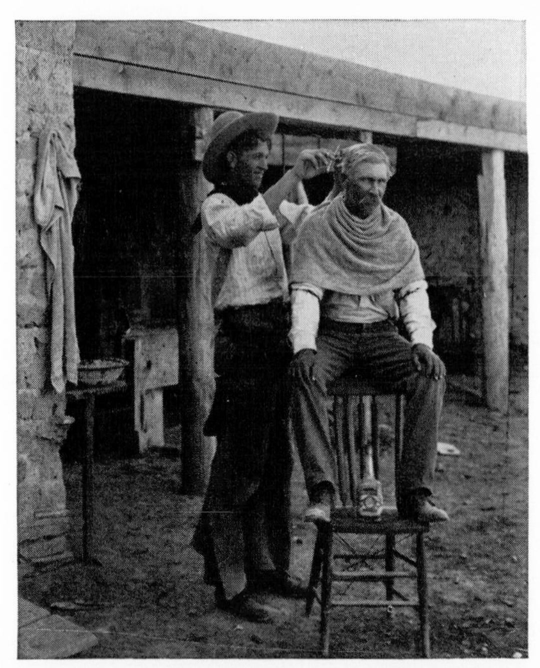

When the fall roundup was over, and the beef cattle had been driven to the nearest railhead for shipment (see preceding page), cowhands began to think about riding into town in search of amusements neither ranch nor range could provide. Haircuts were in order (left; but the bottle on the chair is whiskey, not hair tonic), everyone slicked up, and the spree was on. Old Tascosa, Texas, was the good-time mecca for many of the surrounding ranches, and there Smith recorded the convivial scenes below. After racing the last mile into town to see who would be first at the bar, many of the boys resorted to the entertainment offered down the street by ladies who, if not particularly lovely, thoroughly understood their calling. Back at the ranch (right), a contented cowhand makes a last smoke before turning in for the night.

END OF THE SEASON

"OLD ABE" THE BATTLE EAGLE

COLLECTION OF LESTER S. LEVY

The (mostly) true legend of a Wisconsin outfit's mascot who dodged shells, whined about the chow, and became an honored veteran, living a life of ease at state expense

By BRUCE CATTON

Of all the American eagles ever born in the north woods, the one that came closest to becoming the authentic and accepted National Bird was undoubtedly a fowl named Old Abe. Old Abe was an opinionated and rather self-satisfied creature who seemed quite aware that he was the only eagle in the country to be recognized as a regular veteran of the American Civil War, in which he served as a member of the 8th Wisconsin Volunteer Infantry.

Old Abe put in a full three-year hitch. He was under fire on several occasions—acquitting himself nobly, by all accounts—and when his time expired and he retired he lived the life of Riley, becoming a professional Old Soldier, supported at state expense and enjoying a career of public appearances, banquets, and practically everything except autograph parties. He attended any number of veterans' reunions and county fairs, went to at least one national political convention, and was a featured attraction at the Philadelphia Centennial Exposition of 1876. When he died, full of years and honors, his posthumous fate was like that of no other veteran. He was stuffed and mounted and was maintained for years as a patriotic exhibit.

This eagle was born in the spring of 1861 in a ramshackle nest at the top of a tall pine along the upper reaches of the Flambeau River, in northern Wisconsin. He was still a fledgling when a Chippewa Indian named Chief Sky, spotting the nest from the ground, cut the tree down to see if he could capture an eagle. What Chief Sky got was this one immature bird, untamed, irritable, and full of bitter protests; and a few weeks later, going to the town of Eagle River for supplies, Chief Sky sold the bird to one Daniel McCann for a bushel of corn.

McCann had no especial use for a young eagle, but he figured this was a bargain. A little while after this he went to Chippewa Falls, where a couple of volunteer military units were being organized. He tried to sell the bird to a company which was recruiting for the 1st Wisconsin Artillery, failed, but at last got $2.50 from a local merchant who thought an eagle would be a wonderful mascot for some infantry outfit and who in due course presented the bird, now almost fully grown, to a company known as the "Eau Claire Badgers," which was about to become Company C in the 8th Wisconsin. The soldiers immediately christened their pet "Old Abe," and swore him in by putting a red, white, and blue ribbon about his neck, with a rosette for his bosom.

Old Abe made a hit from the start. A member of the company named James McGinnis was appointed his carrier and caretaker. McGinnis made a perch—a T-shaped affair five feet tall, with small U.S. flags at each end of the crossbar. Old Abe liked this and permitted himself to be carried about on drills and parades. When the Badgers took off for the troop concentration center at Camp Randall they took him along, and were gratified by the number of cheers he got. When they went through La Crosse, Old Abe attracted so much attention that somebody offered the company $250 for him. The offer was spurned, and when the Badgers marched into Camp Randall they knew they had made no mistake; they entered with the band playing "Yankee Doodle," and other recruits swarmed around to see, and Old Abe, doubtless inspired by their cheers, flapped his wings, screamed, and grabbed one of the little flags in his beak, holding it all the way across the camp. This was a good omen, and fine publicity as well; the 8th Wisconsin, when it got organized, was known as the Eagle Regiment, and a fancy new perch was built, with a little Stars and Stripes shield under the crossbar, and clusters of golden arrows at each end of the perch in place of the flags.

McGinnis and his successors found that carrying Abe was no joke, because he was pretty heavy, but by now his adoption was official. One man was formally detailed to the job, with no other assignment. When the regiment was formed in line, for parade, the eagle was always on display just to the left of the color-bearer, in the center of the regiment. The bearer wore a heavy belt with a socket for the lower end of the staff. A leather ring was put around one of Abe's legs, with a twenty-foot cord running from the ring to the staff itself; on parade the surplus cord was wound about the perch so that Abe would stay put.

When the regiment went through Chicago on its way to the war, Old Abe excited the spectators just as he had done at Camp Randall. In St. Louis, however, his

CONTINUED ON PAGE 106

LIBRARY OF CONGRESS

Whenever the 8th Wisconsin paraded, Old Abe marched with the color guard. Here they form up at Vicksburg in 1863.

The song tells of John Henry, steel-drivin' man, who fought a steam drill and won. Did he? Or was he just a myth?

ROBERT WEAVER

"A man ain't nothin' but a man"

By BERNARD ASBELL

We often describe our neglected heroes as "unsung," but surely the most "sung" hero in American history—taking the adjective literally—is a legendary Negro laborer from West Virginia named John Henry.

Nine tenths of all American Negroes, it has been said, are familiar with the "Ballad of John Henry" in some form; those who don't know the song can tell its story. Among white people, too, the song has spread widely, particularly among railroad workers in the Southeast and coal miners in West Virginia and Kentucky, each group claiming John Henry as one of its own. Some of them have been known to resent the suggestion that John Henry was a Negro. He has been geographically claimed by Virginia, the Carolinas, Kentucky, Tennessee, Alabama, and Louisiana, and probably lots more. Like many other folk characters, John Henry assumes the image of those who sing about him.

Among professional musicians too, the ballad—without benefit of payola and promotion—has enjoyed a curious popularity. In supper clubs, urbane folk singers perform it for urbane diners. In the recital hall, Richard Dyer-Bennet clips it out in British accents. Aaron Copland has composed an orchestral suite based on it. Even a modern jazz band, the Sauter-Finegan Orchestra, has recorded it as a rhythmic recitation. The song seems to get newer and fresher, or at least more popular, all the time.

It would be tempting to say that the ballad's popularity owes itself to the brilliance of its tune and the power of its words. But this cannot truthfully be said. Hardly any two singers sing the song to the same melody. Similarly, they vary the wording of its verses. The appeal of the legend, therefore, must be in the lean, muscular characterization of John Henry and the event that immortalized him.

John Henry was born to die with a hammer in his hand. (According to many versions of the tall tale, he announced this destiny to his mother when he was only three days old.) He grew up to become a great steel driver at Big Bend Tunnel on the Chesapeake and Ohio Railroad. A steel driver was a man who hammered a steel rod into rock to make holes for inserting explosives. One day, his foreman, or "captain," introduced a steam drill, whereupon:

John Henry told his captain
"A man ain't nothin' but a man,
But before I let your steam drill beat me down,
I'll die with a hammer in my hand, Lord, Lord,
I'll die with a hammer in my hand."

His dignity at stake, John Henry challenged the steam drill to a race. He pounded "until his hammer was strikin' fire," and drove an accumulated length of fourteen feet of steel, while the steam drill only made nine. Then, asking for a cool drink of water, he lay down his hammer and he died. He was given a hero's burial:

They took John Henry to the White House
And buried him in the sand,
Every locomotive come a-roarin' by
Cried "Yonder lies a steel-drivin' man, Lord, Lord,
Yonder lies a steel-drivin' man."

When that tribute is not contained in a particular version of the song, often this one is:

When John Henry died there was no coffin
Big enough to hold all his bones,
So they put him in a box car and buried him
in the ground
And let a mountain be his gravestone, Lord, Lord,
Let a mountain be his gravestone.

Nobody knows today who wrote the song. In fact, "wrote" may be the wrong verb, for the man who was first moved to sing about John Henry perhaps never wrote down his words at all. The earliest-known copies of the ballad, in the form of cheaply produced broadsides, are believed to have been printed about the turn of the century, when the legend had already been widely diffused.

"John Henry" is truly a folk song. It was kept alive, at least in its early years, by one singer learning it from another. Singers have changed it to suit their musical and poetic tastes, or remade it to fill in for their failing memories. Thus they evolved it into a new, bigger, more dramatic story—indeed, a tall story. As a succession of nameless guitarists and banjo-pickers got further and further from the facts, they turned more and more to artistic invention.

The poem they have left us, of a proud hammer-swinger caught in a conflict of the industrial revolution, resembles classic tragedy. Our hero's destiny is prophesied before his journey begins. Then, threatened by the machine, he meets the challenge, defeats the machine in a race, and pays for his victory with his life. We do not know, when the song ends, whether to exult or to weep. As in classic tragedy, we are not quite sure if the hero has won or lost.

What makes John Henry so attractive a literary and historical character? Did he ever live? Did he race a steam drill? Did he beat it and, if so, did his victory destroy him? Why has his story survived? It seems in order to look first at what is known of the facts.

When the tracks of the Chesapeake and Ohio Railway first stretched westward through Virginia and then, in the closing months of the 1860's, crossed the West Virginia line, the engineers collided with the most formidable of their natural obstacles, the Allegheny Mountains.

More than two years were consumed merely in surveying the wilderness from White Sulphur Springs, on the state line, to Kanawha Falls, little more than fifty miles westward. Surveyors followed what appeared to be the course of least resistance, the banks of the Greenbrier; but the river, wrenching and twisting like an angry snake, lent little ease to their task.

Half a mile west of Talcott in Summers County, the Greenbrier turns to the south. It wanders for about ten miles in a near loop, doubling back almost to where the bend begins—only a little more than a mile west. Engineers had to decide either to lay their track along the winding riverbank or to tunnel a mile and a quarter through the red shale mountain. They decided to tunnel. It was a decision of great magnitude, for the tunnel was to be, at that time, the longest in America.

The first chip in the mountainside was hammered early in 1870. Late in 1872, the bore was completed, trackage laid, and the first train passed through. Over the portals, in stone lettering, the men carved the name, Great Bend Tunnel. But then and now, everybody has always called it the Big Bend.

About a thousand men labored in Big Bend Tunnel. Most of them were Negroes, only seven or eight years out of slavery. Nobody knows how many of them died, for there seemed to be a studied effort on the part of both the railroad and the press to play down the casualties. If the danger became too widely known, labor might become too difficult to recruit. But guesses might be based on casualties reported at other tunnels. The Wheeling *Intelligencer* said on December 30, 1870, that 1,000 lives had been lost at Mont Cenis Tunnel in the French Alps. The Kanawha *Chronicle* revealed on December 17, 1873, that 136 had been killed in boring Hoosac Tunnel in Massachusetts.

The three great killers were tunnel sickness (from heat and foul air), explosives (nitroglycerin, dualin, and gunpowder), and falls of rock. At Big Bend, one slide of 8,000 cubic feet of rock was reported by the Greenbrier *Independent* on June 1, 1872, but the paper said nothing about casualties. Many must have been dead by then, however, for as the tunnel penetrated the mountain, the likelihood of deaths from foul air mounted with each day.

And constantly there was the blasting of explosives. Drilling in Mont Cenis Tunnel was described in *Every Saturday*, October 14, 1871: "The smoke from the blast became so thick that the light from the lamps was visible no farther than a few steps . . . Suddenly an infernal noise burst upon us from the end of the gallery. One would have said ten thousand hammers were falling simultaneously on their anvils. A sharp, whistling sound made itself heard above this clamor, piercing you to the very marrow."

Under conditions such as these, men like John Henry labored at Big Bend for twelve to fourteen hours a day to do what the engineers said had to be done. America needed a new railroad to move west, and a mountain was standing in the way.

In the middle and late 1920's, while there was still time to locate living persons who might have been on hand at the building of Big Bend Tunnel, a pair of folklorists became interested in John Henry and his exploits. These two men conducted their investigations separately—in fact, competitively—and with occasional flares of animosity. But their research uncovered virtually all the reliable material. Guy B. Johnson, of the University of North Carolina Institute for Research in Social Science, published his findings in 1928 (*John Henry: Tracking Down a Negro Legend*). Louis W. Chappell, associate professor of English, University of West Virginia, published his in 1933 (*John Henry: A Folklore Study*).

The first step in pursuit of the legend was to find out whether John Henry's race against the steam drill *could* have taken place. This meant establishing whether both hand labor and steam drilling were practiced while Big Bend Tunnel was under construction; and then, whether the race described in the ballad would have been a reasonable contest.

If a drill was tried at the east portal of Big Bend, as claimed in certain testimony gathered by Johnson and Chappell, it would have been used early in the two years of east-to-west construction, probably in the summer or fall of 1870.

The first reciprocating percussion drill was apparently patented in March, 1849, by J. J. Couch of Philadelphia. A steam drill was used in the construction of Hoosac Tunnel, which was begun in 1855 and completed in 1873. Another was used at Lewis Tunnel, a few miles from Big Bend, in January, November, and possibly in April of 1871. While Lewis was cut mainly through hard sandstone, Big Bend had to be drilled through red shale. A drill might suit one and not the other. But if a drill manufacturer sold one to the contractor at Lewis, it seems likely he would have tried to make another sale at Big Bend.

But the facts of the John Henry legend, it appears, were fated to elude historians. While there is an abundance of data about other tunnels, a fire in a Chesapeake & Ohio warehouse destroyed all the engineers' and contractors' reports about Big Bend. All must rest on recollection and hearsay.

One of the few living men found by Johnson who had anything to do with the engineering aspects of Big Bend was a Chesapeake & Ohio engineer named James P. Nelson, who said: "I saw the first shovelful of earth cast, and worked on top of the tunnel and underneath it, day and night, and have no recollection of a steam drill having been used."

Johnson also located William Wimmer, a retired locomotive engineer living near the tunnel, who claimed that he had driven the first locomotive through Big Bend. He was seventy-two when Johnson interviewed him; he had been fourteen when work began on the tunnel. Wimmer said:

"I carried water and steel to shaft number one. That was down toward the west end of the tunnel. I have heard about the steel-driving contest but I think I must have heard about it some time after the tunnel was finished." But a race could have taken place at the east end, Wimmer allowed, without his hearing of it.

> You see, those steel-driving contests were pretty common. I don't mean between men and steam drills, but between two pair of drivers. I have seen many a contest in my day. Back in North Carolina, I've seen two or three hundred people gather on a Sunday afternoon to see a contest. There'd usually be a wager up. They'd agree to drive a certain depth or a certain length of time and the winning pair, that is, the driver and the turner, would get the money. I've seen them put up two or three hundred dollars in a contest—besides lots of bets by spectators on the side. Most people who have worked around tunnels or quarries get used to contests and sort of take them for granted; so I can see how this fellow, John Henry, could have had his contest without raising much stir around camp. Still, since it was a man against a steam drill, it does look as if the news would have spread around pretty well.

The "news," in fact, did spread pretty well. Around Talcott and the Summers County seat, Hinton, the investigations of Johnson and Chappell turned up several elderly Negroes who claimed to have known John Henry himself. Nearly every one of them professed absolute knowledge that the race took place, but in every case their accounts collapsed under scrutiny. The informants would relate John Henry to the wrong dates or the wrong contractor or even the wrong tunnel. But the tale had persisted among them.

Two bits of hearsay picked up by Chappell, both from old-time white residents of the area, suggest that the race was known and discussed by John Henry's contemporaries. One was J. E. Huston, who began work as a telegrapher at Big Bend in 1893. He said:

The John Henry story has been in our family ever since we moved to Big Bend Tunnel in 1881. My father worked for the C&O Railroad and they moved him to Talcott in 1881. After we moved here I heard him talk with people around the tunnel time and time again about the contest John Henry had with the steam drill.

The other account came from George Hedrick, who was seventeen when work began on Big Bend in 1870. He lived a few hundred yards from the tunnel with his brother, John, twenty-three, and their father. He told Chappell:

My brother John helped to survey the tunnel and had charge of the woodwork in building it. I often saw John Henry drive steel out there. I saw the steam drill too, when they brought it to the east end of the tunnel, but I didn't see John Henry when he drove in the contest with it. I heard about it right after. My brother saw it. My memory is Bill Henderson and John Henry drove together against the steam drill. That was the usual way of driving steel in the tunnel.

George Hedrick added that John Henry "was black, and six feet high, thirty-five years old and weighed two hundred or a little more. He could sing as well as he could drive steel and was always singing when he was in the tunnel—'Can't you drive her—huh!' "

An interview with his brother, John Hedrick, revealed that he didn't quite see the race either:

I was manager of the woodwork in putting through Big Bend Tunnel and built the shanties of the Negroes there in the camp . . . He [John Henry] drove steel with the steam drill at the east end of the inside of the tunnel not far from the end. He was working under Foreman Steele and he beat the steam drill, too. The steam drill got hung up, but John Henry was beating him all the time. I didn't see the contest, because it was on the inside of the tunnel and not many could get in there. I was taking up timber and heard him singing and driving and he was keeping in tune.

The man who came closest to being an eyewitness of the race, at least according to his own claim, was C. S. "Neal" Miller, who came to the Big Bend Tunnel area in the spring of 1869 at the age of seventeen. As a water boy and steel carrier for the drivers at the east end, Miller claimed he carried for the gang of which John Henry was a member:

I saw John Henry drive steel in Big Bend Tunnel. He was a great singer, and always singing some old song when he was driving steel. He was a black, raw-boned man, thirty years old, six feet high and weighed near two hundred pounds. He and Phil Henderson, another big Negro but not so high, were pals, and said that they were from North Carolina . . . Dave Withrow, who lived with his wife at our home, was foreman in charge of the work on the outside of the tunnel where John Henry beat the steam drill, and Mike Breen was the foreman on the inside of the tunnel there.

The steam drill was brought to Big Bend Tunnel as an experiment, and failed because it stayed broke all the time, or hung up in the rocks, and it could be used only on bench drills anyway. It was brought to the east end of the tunnel when work first commenced there, and was never carried in the tunnel. It was thrown aside, and the engine was taken from it and carried to shaft number one, where it took the place of a team of horses and pulled the bucket up in the shaft with a windlass.

When Johnson asked Miller if the contest had many witnesses or had caused excitement, Miller replied:

No, it was just considered a sort of test on the steam drill. There wasn't any big crowd around to see it. I was going and coming with water and steel, so I saw how they were getting along from time to time. But I didn't get excited over it especially. The test lasted over a part of two days, and the depth was twenty feet, more or less.

An intriguing item in Miller's testimony is that he recalls the event not as a race but a *test*. Thus, by reducing the tale's drama, he increases its plausibility. A sales demonstration of a machine previously sold, say, to the contractor of Lewis Tunnel, would not be likely to whip up a crowd as a race would. Also, the foreman would in all likelihood have hushed up the event so as not to divert other laborers from their jobs. And finally, if the machine failed, as Miller says it did, the maker of the steam drill would be even less likely to have mentioned the test.

But if the machine was useful at other tunnels, would it fail at Big Bend? Johnson learned from a Mr. Walter Jordan of New York, who, he said, "has had a long acquaintance with drills and drillers," that a steam drill would break down in certain kinds of rock. Neal Miller's firsthand recollection of the machine's failure fits neatly with this statement from Jordan:

The writer has himself often beat a steam drill or air drill on a down [wet] hole in very soft rock, as the machine would "mud up" and have to be cleaned every four or five inches. I have often seen a churn drill out a hole in soft rock where it would be impossible to use a machine.

The ballad itself rephrases the testimony of Walter Jordan and Neal Miller, as though the singers have known that Big Bend was cut through red shale instead of hard sandstone:

John Henry told his captain
"Oh, captain, can't you see
Your hole's done choked and your drill's done broke
And it can't drive steel like me, Lord, Lord,
No, it can't drive steel like me."

CONTINUED ON PAGE 95

What the Supreme Court wrought: Within fifteen years after Gibbons v. Ogden, *the steamboat was fast becoming queen of the rive*

GIBBONS
v.
OGDEN

The Steamboat's

COLLECTION OF WILLIAM L. HOPKINS, JR.

Thomas Gibbons, by an unknown artist

The famous case of *Gibbons v. Ogden,* decided on March 2, 1824, was, with its preceding litigation, ultimately concerned with a single question: the power of Congress to regulate interstate as well as foreign commerce. It produced a triumph for nationalism, in the most generous and constructive sense of that term, and its influence has been immense. Its immediate effect, however, was to release from monopoly, like a genie from a bottle, a sooty, romantic, and useful servant to the American people—the steamboat.

One cannot altogether understand this aspect of *Gibbons v. Ogden* without considering the origins and consequences of the Livingston-Fulton steamboat monopoly and the personalities involved in them: personalities of considerable determination and marked eccentricity, one of whom was brushed with genius.

The actual inaugurators of the American steamboat—John Fitch, James Rumsey, and perhaps Oliver Evans—were also its innocent victims; they could make it run, but they could not make it run economically, nor could they raise sufficient funds

Robert Havell's 1839 aquatint shows traffic on the Hudson River—once the private preserve of Fulton and Livingston—off Manhattan.

Charter of Freedom

By GEORGE DANGERFIELD

to enable them, by research and experiment, to overcome this problem. One still sees them, nobly (and in Fitch's case somewhat drunkenly) silhouetted against the pale dawn of the age of steam, gesticulating in vain to the inattentive financier, the jocose and skeptical public. From their valiant dust springs *Gibbons v. Ogden*.

The great case may be taken back to March 27, 1798, when the New York legislature repealed an exclusive privilege to run steamboats on state waters, which it had conferred on John Fitch, and bestowed it instead upon Robert R. Livingston, chancellor of the state. Livingston had what Fitch conspicuously lacked—social status, political influence, wealth, credit. He resembled Fitch only in one respect: he was an enthusiast. An amateur scientist, he believed that nature might at any moment yield one of her tremendous secrets to some chance experiment or happy flash of insight. The building of gristmills on a novel principle to eliminate friction between the stones; the crossing of cows with the elk in his park at Clermont on the Hudson;

NEW-YORK HISTORICAL SOCIETY

Aaron Ogden, by Asher B. Durand

WEBB INSTITUTE OF NAVAL ARCHITECTURE

The painting above, by an unknown artist, shows Robert Fulton (right) explaining his first steamboat plan to his backer, Robert R. Livingston. The famous result of their collaboration was the ship called by the public (but never by its builders) the Clermont, *seen below in a charming—if not technically accurate—French lithograph. Given a monopoly by New York State, they achieved what had eluded equally deserving steamboat inventors—commercial success.*

ABOVE AND PAGES 38–39 TOP, NEW YORK PUBLIC LIBRARY, PHELPS STOKES COLLECTION the manufacture of paper out of river-weed locally known as frog's spit—such schemes and fancies occupied his leisure hours.

His spirit, one might almost say, dwelt more and more apart on the farthest and most aery borders of rational speculation: almost but not quite. He was a progressive farmer, for example, whose work was of the first importance. And there was a hard, practical element in his singular composition—he was, after all, of Scottish and Dutch descent—which made it unlikely that he would throw good money after bad. To his great credit, he had perceived that the steamboat had a future: and although steamboat legislation, like Vulcan among the gods, excited the immortal laughter of the New York legislature, Livingston was quite impervious to mockery of this sort.

His experiments with John Stevens (one of the fathers of the railroad) and Nicholas J. Roosevelt proved abortive; and when he left for France in 1801, where as American minister he plunged into those complex and exasperating negotiations which ultimately led to the purchase of Louisiana, it was presumed that no more would be heard of the steamboat. But in Paris he met the one man who could give his schemes what they needed—precision, economy, practicability.

Robert Fulton, darkly handsome, supremely self-confident, the very embodiment of energy, had been raised as an artisan in Lancaster, Pennsylvania. He had been a locksmith, a gunsmith, a draughtsman, a portrait painter; he had gone to England to study under Benjamin West; and in England he had first conceived what was to become a permanent preoccupation with submarines and submarine torpedoes. Of Fulton it might indeed be doubted whether his lifelong purpose was to put boats upon the water or to blow them out of it.

One thing, however, was certain. He had, supremely, the faculty of co-ordination. Other men's original ideas, in the realm of steamboats, existed only to be borrowed: "All these things," he said airily, "being governed by the laws of nature, the real invention is to find [such laws]." To him, it was all a matter of exact proportions, of nicely calculated relations. Where the steamboat was concerned, it was Fulton's destiny, and his genius, to find a commotion and to turn it into a revolution.

Fulton and Livingston put an experimental steamboat upon the Seine; its performance satisfied them, and Fulton left for England to cajole out of the British government a Boulton & Watt engine built to his own specifications. The engine was claimed by Fulton from the New York Customs House on April 23, 1807; it was placed in a boat built at the Charles Brownne shipyards at Paulus Hook; and on August 17, 1807, *The Steamboat* (her builders never seemed to have called her the *Clermont*) made her triumphant voyage from New York to Albany.*

On her maiden night, as she passed through the darkling highlands of the Hudson, a plangent volcano, the steamboat excited great terror among the pious dwellers beside the banks of that river. One rustic is said to have raced home, barred the doors, and shouted that the devil himself was going up to Albany in a sawmill.

Here he was, from any point of view, wrong. It was not a demon; it was a most useful spirit that had been released by Fulton and Livingston: the trouble was that, having released it, they at once imprisoned it again. Fulton did indeed take out two United States patents—perhaps more interesting as essays than valid as claims—but it was not upon these that he and Livingston relied: their great support was restrictive state legislation.

On April 6, 1808, the New York legislature extended their privilege up to a limit of thirty years and imposed thumping penalties on anyone who dared, without a license from the monopoly, to navigate by steam upon any of the waters of New York. In 1809, a sister ship, the *Car of Neptune,* was built; in 1810, the *Paragon* appeared; on April 9, 1811, the New York legislature passed a monopoly act even more stringent in its penalties than the one enacted in 1808. And in April, 1811, the legislature of the Territory of Orleans conferred upon Livingston and Fulton privileges fully as extensive as those granted by New York. Thus they controlled two of the greatest commercial waterways in the United States.

Although they had shown true vision in their estimate of the steamboat's future, Livingston and Fulton had been somewhat less perceptive in gauging the reaction of their countrymen. They had not supposed that their monopoly would be unpopular, still less that it would be seriously resisted. From the outset, however, obloquy and litigation became their portion. The litigation reached its climax in 1811, when twenty-one enterprising gentlemen of Albany started a rival steamboat, the *Hope,* upon the Albany-New York run, and threatened to follow her up with a sister ship, not inaptly to be called the *Perseverance.*

The monopolists, of course, fought back in the courts, and in March, 1812, New York's Chief Justice

* Fulton variously referred to the vessel as the *North River Steamboat of Clermont*—after Livingston's Hudson estate—the *North River Steamboat,* or the *North River.* On her first voyage, she seems simply to have been *The Steamboat.* But the public came to call her the *Clermont,* and the name stuck.

James Kent issued a permanent injunction against the *Hope*. Kent's very learned opinion may be reduced to this simple proposition: either the New York steamboat acts violated the federal Constitution or they did not. A stern supporter of states' rights, Kent ruled that they did not. Obviously, he said, where a national and a state law are aimed against each other, the state law must yield. But this was not the case here, since all commerce within a state was exclusively within the power of that state. Supported by Kent, one of the most respected jurists in the nation, the monopoly had certainly become respectable. When Robert R. Livingston, full of years and honors, died in 1813, when Robert Fulton followed him into the shades in 1815, they left to their heirs and assigns an inheritance as rich and safe as state laws could make it.

Nonetheless, the contentious atmosphere which had clouded the monopoly from the beginning seems to have been increased rather than diminished by the decision of Kent. New Jersey had already passed a retaliatory act in 1811; in the course of time her example was followed by Connecticut and Ohio. Massachusetts, Georgia, New Hampshire, Vermont, and Pennsylvania bestowed exclusive rights upon their own favored monopolists. Elsewhere, unlicensed steamboats blew their lonely, defiant whistles upon remote lakes and waterways, while denizens of the uncharted wilderness crept down to watch and wonder.

The development of the steamboat was a great adventure, but it was threatening to provoke a commercial civil war—unless, indeed, someone could break the Livingston-Fulton grip upon Louisiana and New York. In the former state, by 1819, there were distinct signs of rebellion; but the latter, the cradle of the whole restrictive movement, would undoubtedly prove to be the most dramatic and decisive scene for some abrupt reversal of this ominous trend. . . .

In May, 1819, John R. Livingston of New York brought suit in the Chancery Court of that state against Aaron Ogden and Thomas Gibbons of New Jersey. Mr. Livingston, a younger brother of Robert R. Livingston, was a wealthy merchant who had dedicated his youth to making what he called "something clever" out of the Revolution and who had thereafter devoted his energies to the single-minded pursuit of material advantage. In 1808, for the extremely stiff price of one-sixth of his gross proceeds, he had purchased from his brother's monopoly the exclusive right to navigate steamboats "from any place within the city of New York lying south of the State Prison to the Jersey shore and Staten Island, viz.: Staten Island, Elizabethtown Point, Amboy and the Raritan up to Brunswick, but to no place or point north of Powles Hook." (The location of Powles, or Paulus, Hook may be determined by drawing a line from the southernmost tip of Manhattan Island due west to the Jersey shore.) He was certain to extract from this hard-bought concession whatever there was to be extracted—and thus arose his suit against Ogden and Gibbons.

Aaron Ogden, finding the New Jersey legislature unwilling to support him in his claim to run steamboats on his own, had reluctantly yielded to the monopoly in 1815, and had purchased from Mr. Livingston, its assignee, the right to run a steamboat ferry from Elizabethtown Point to New York. A Revolutionary soldier who had fought at Yorktown, a former governor of New Jersey, and one of the state's leading lawyers and most prominent Federalists, Ogden was a man of impressive physique, craggy and truculent countenance, and character to match. He bore the monopoly no good will, and in the course of time he acquired in Thomas Gibbons a partner even more contentious than himself.

Gibbons was a wealthy lawyer from Georgia who had acquired a home in Elizabethtown, New Jersey, in 1811. He had been a Loyalist during the Revolution, thereby (since his brother and father were both patriots) saving the family plantation from both British vandalism and anti-Loyalist revenge. His was not exactly a happy record, but he had survived it, to acquire at length a reputation, notable even in Georgia, for some of the more opprobrious and quarrelsome forms of political meddling. "His soul," said one enemy, "is faction and his life has been a scene of political corruption."

The partnership between Ogden and Gibbons, instituted in 1817, was no doubt doomed from the start. In October, 1818, Ogden obtained an injunction against Gibbons in the New York Chancery Court, presumably because that oblique personage could not resist the temptation to cheat his partner by running a steamboat on his own account from Paulus Hook to New York. Nonetheless, when John R. Livingston brought suit against the pair in 1819, their partnership was still uneasily alive upon the following terms: Ogden ran passengers from New York to Elizabethtown Point in his steamboat *Atalanta*. At Elizabethtown Point, the passengers changed into Gibbons' *Bellona*, for which (as for his smaller steamboat, the *Stoudinger*) Gibbons had taken out a United States coasting license. The passengers were then carried to New Brunswick, from whence they proceeded overland to Trenton and Philadelphia.

John R. Livingston, whose steamboat *Olive Branch* ran regularly from New York to New Brunswick, claimed that the Ogden-Gibbons partnership constituted a single voyage, in defiance of his exclusive right.

METROPOLITAN MUSEUM OF ART, ROGERS FUND, 1942

The Paragon, *another steamboat built by Livingston and Fulton for the Hudson run, was the subject of a water color done about 1811 by a Russian traveller, Paul Svinin. Evidently he found the passengers as novel as the ship itself, for he wrote of the deck life: "Here you see a happy pair of lovers, near them a politician absorbed in the newspapers: there people play chess; in another place a Federalist is arguing hotly with a Democrat, to the sound of a flute or guitar played by a neighbor; in a corner there is a greedy money-chaser annoyed by the children whose clamor distracts him from his accounts; finally dogs and cats add to the fascination . . . It is not a house, but a whole floating town!"*

He also showed that the partners had a common booking agent in New York, one William B. Jaques. Livingston sought an injunction restraining them from navigating their two boats, except from New York to Elizabethtown Point. This meant that in future the *Atalanta* would have to transfer her passengers, not into Gibbons' *Bellona,* but into Livingston's *Olive Branch.*

Both Gibbons and Ogden disclaimed any partnership or any knowledge of Mr. Jaques. Both insisted that the ports and harbors of Elizabethtown Point and New Brunswick were within the jurisdiction of New Jersey, as were the waters lying between them; and both asserted that the agreement between the monopoly and John R. Livingston gave the latter no right whatsoever to navigate between a port in New York and one in New Jersey. Gibbons had other arguments, but the chief of them—and this in time became the crux of the whole matter—was that under his national coasting license he had a perfect right to navigate between one point in New Jersey and another.

The reigning chancellor of New York was now none other than James Kent, who, as chief justice, had delivered the decisive opinion in the case of the *Hope* in 1812. That he would reverse in the Court of Chancery a decision he had delivered in the Court of Errors was not to be expected. In a complicated decision that adds nothing to his fame as a jurist, he held that Ogden could continue to steam between New York and Elizabethtown Point in the *Atalanta,* but that Gibbons' *Bellona* could not operate between the Point and New Brunswick.

If the temperaments of Ogden and Gibbons had been more compatible, they might have continued the fight together. The New York law, claiming jurisdiction all the way to the Jersey shore, was clearly preposterous, and simple justice should have compelled the partners to stand together for their common rights. But Ogden decided to content himself with Kent's decision. No doubt he contemplated the discomfiture of Gibbons with a certain amount of ill-concealed complacency.

The result was the final break between Gibbons and Ogden. Gibbons was justifiably angry and full of fight. Because Kent had ignored his federal coasting license argument, he decided to bring the case to the United States Supreme Court. Meanwhile he hoped to stir up

CONTINUED ON PAGE 78

When Boston's police walked out, a great city erupted in violence

The Strike That Made a President

By FRANCIS RUSSELL

BOSTON *Globe*

The Law takes a holiday: *On September 8, 1919, defiant Boston policemen file out from the meeting where their final decision to strike was made. The vote was 1,134 to 2.*

Had it not been for the Boston police strike of September, 1919, Calvin Coolidge probably would have become just another in the succession of Republican governors of Massachusetts, his name no more remembered than that of his predecessor, Samuel McCall, or his successor, Channing Cox. But the curious and chance circumstances of that event suddenly made him known all over America. To the rest of the country Coolidge became a courageous Yankee figure of the minuteman stamp who had defied and defeated the violence that had threatened the seventh city of the United States.

For two days the central core of Boston with its more than 700,000 inhabitants was without police protection, and the mob ruled the streets. Ordinary Bostonians were as shocked by this savagery as they were dismayed to find how thin was the veneer of legal restraint by which they had ordered their lives. Conservatives like Henry Cabot Lodge saw the strike as a first step toward sovietizing the country. The striking policemen, most of whom were Irish and Catholic by descent, would have been astonished at any such notion. They were ordinary Americans with an immediate grievance so engrossing that they gave little thought to the consequences of their protest.

In the larger analysis the strike was part of the general pattern of industrial unrest that accompanied the dislocations of the postwar period; 1919 was a year of strikes—the great steel strike, the Seattle general strike, railways and transit strikes, a coal strike, longshoremen's strikes, strikes of actors in New York, even a buyers' strike. Their immediate common cause was in-

y doggedly doing nothing, Governor Coolidge emerged as a national hero

BROWN BROTHERS

UPI

BROWN BROTHERS

Passing the buck: *Each of these men had the power to prevent the strike, and failed to exercise it. From left to right are Andrew J. Peters, the inept Democratic mayor; Edwin U. Curtis, the police commissioner whose refusal to compromise precipitated the walk-out; and Calvin Coolidge, the Republican governor, who acted only after the strike was broken—and then got all the credit.*

flation and the failure of wages to keep up with the high cost of living. The underlying cause was, however, that anti-climactic restlessness that runs through every society following the artificial unity of a war.

As for the policemen's grievances, they were real enough. In spite of a slight raise their minimum pay was $1,100 a year—less than half what many a war worker had been earning—and out of this they had to buy their uniforms. Beyond the question of pay was an even larger grievance: a two-platoon system that kept the men on twelve-hour shifts. Station houses were old, crowded, and dirty. To the ordinary Boston patrolman a union seemed the answer. Not only had the Boston firemen formed one without causing any comment or protest, but police in thirty-seven other American cities already had unions.

The Boston police strike was not unique. Many other police strikes before and since have been passed over and forgotten. In Boston, though, there was no one to replace the police when they struck. That the city was left without protection was the fault of Police Commissioner Edwin U. Curtis. Indirectly Mayor Andrew J. Peters and Governor Coolidge also shared the responsibility. Ironically enough, Coolidge, who did the least, received the final credit for doing everything.

Twenty-four years before becoming police commissioner, Curtis had been at the age of thirty-four the youngest mayor the city of Boston had ever had. He came from an established and wealthy family, and he felt that in taking public office again he was doing his duty to the community and to his country. His position as commissioner was anomalous. A generation before, when he was mayor, the old-line Bostonians who had governed the city since the Revolution still controlled the city they considered theirs by inheritance. But even then they were being pushed by the Irish offspring of the famine years. When it became obvious that Irish Democrats would take over Boston politically, the Republican state legislature engineered a law to place the appointment of the Boston police commissioner in the hands of the governor. Thus, while the Jim Curleys might possess City Hall, they would not be able to get their fingers on the police department.

Curtis in his middle age had become an autocratic Puritan with supercilious eyes and a puffy, disdainful face. His attitude toward the police was that of a general toward his troops. They were "his" men, and in the hierarchy of command his orders were to be obeyed cheerfully and without question. At the core of Curtis' unbending personality was a sense of insecurity occasioned by the social changes on the Boston scene. He despised and feared the newly emerging Irish, with their alien religion and their eye for political plunder. In his heart he was convinced that Boston would never again be a decent city until the ephemeral Honey Fitzes and Jim Curleys and Dan Coakleys had been replaced by Curtises. That was why in the period of Boston's political decline he had accepted the office of police commissioner from Governor McCall.

During the early summer months of 1919 the policemen began organizing themselves into an unofficial union, the Boston Social Club. Curtis countered with a general order stating that for a police officer union

***Mob rule:** Scollay Square, center of the rioting, was a sinister scene as the crowds broke windows and looted shops.*

membership was inconsistent with the performance of his sworn duty. In spite of this warning the Boston Social Club applied for a charter from the American Federation of Labor.

Curtis at once announced an addition to his departmental rules and regulations. From then on, stated Section 19, Rule 35: "No members of the force shall join or belong to any organization, club or body outside the department."

On August 11 the American Federation of Labor granted a charter to the Social Club as Boston Police Union, No. 16,807. Curtis proceeded to charge the eight leaders and officers of the new union with insubordination and ordered them placed on departmental trial. The union countered by warning him that if these men were disciplined the police would strike. The union also maintained that Curtis's regulation was "invalid, unreasonable and contrary to the express law of Massachusetts." Curtis found the men guilty but postponed sentence. On August 29 he found eleven more leaders guilty but again suspended sentence—to give the men a chance to withdraw from the Federation, he later claimed. He then announced that he would pass sentence on September 4. This was the impasse at the end of August.

No one was more distressed at the prospect of a police strike than the mayor of Boston, Andrew J. Peters. By nature Peters was a more conciliatory type than the Commissioner. In addition, he belonged to the same political party as the policemen. He was that rarity, a Yankee Democrat. Here and there they were to be found in Massachusetts, of colonial descent, of inherited wealth, Harvard-educated, and yet by some twist of family allegiance standing outside the old Bay State Federalist tradition. President emeritus Charles W. Eliot of Harvard was such a Democrat, as were the Russells of Cambridge; Winslow Warren, the President of the Society of the Cincinnati and a descendant of the Bunker Hill general; and ex-Governor Eugene Noble Foss.

Peters was an interim mayor between the first and second administrations of the flamboyant James Michael Curley. He had been elected with the help of the Good Government Association—Goo-goos to Jim Curley—while Curley and Congressman James Gallivan were at each other's political throats.

***Delayed protection:** Only on the second day of the strike were militiamen called to guard stores and quell disorder.*

To the more optimistic old Bostonians Peters had seemed a sign of the city's redemption. The new mayor was in the Social Register, he was wealthy enough to be personally honest, and he was conciliatory, as befitted a Democrat. Unfortunately he was also ineffectual. In Woodrow Wilson's first administration he had served casually as Assistant Secretary of the Treasury. In Boston he was lost. While he sat in the mayor's office, bagmen did business in the anterooms, and greenbacks were passed routinely in the corridors. Under the rule of John F. "Honey" Fitzgerald, mayor in 1906–7 and 1910–14, contractors had a habit of charging the city for each side of a granite paving block; under Peters they sold the foundations of City Hall.

Peters resembled an aberrant Scot more than a Yankee. He had a high forehead fringed by rufous hair that gave him the spurious look of a thinker, and curiously tufted, almost Mephistophelian eyebrows. He spoke in a high voice with a precise, exaggerated Harvard accent.

Politics was an avocation rather than a vocation with him: he preferred golf and yachting to long hours at his desk. Somehow he was able to shut both his mind and his eyes to the corruption of his administration. He gave the impression of an easy, superficial man, inclined to bore.

With dazed impotence, Mayor Peters watched the August days recede. The threat of the coming strike was too much for him, and like other weak men in a crisis he looked for some means of shifting responsibility. The safest and easiest way was, as always, to appoint a committee. So in the last week of the month the Mayor named a Citizens' Committee of Thirty-Four to investigate and advise on the situation in the police department. The group was made up of old Bostonians, with a lacing of wealthy Irish and Jewish merchants. It was headed by James J. Storrow of the brokerage firm of Lee, Higginson & Company.

At the outset the committee opposed the police affiliation with the American Federation of Labor. Except for this, they felt a compromise could be worked out if Curtis did not force the issue. From August 29 to September 2 they met daily with the president and leaders of the Police Union. But the chief obstacle to any settlement was the Commissioner, whose adamant stand only stiffened the intransigence of the police.

Volunteers: *Department-store owner John Shepard, Jr. (center) and two aides struck a resolute pose with loaded guns.*

On Wednesday, September 3, he refused Storrow's request for a few days' delay in passing sentence on the leaders of the Police Union, but when Peters made the request formal, Curtis finally agreed to put off his decision until the following Monday.

Meanwhile Governor Coolidge sat aloof in his Statehouse office two hundred yards from City Hall. At this point, as Claude M. Fuess in his definitive life of Coolidge admits, "A single word from him [Coolidge] would probably have led to a compromise, but that word he would not utter."

William Allen White in *A Puritan in Babylon* tells the story of Calvin Coolidge as a student at Black River Academy. Calvin was in bed one evening in the dormitory while several other boys of more prankish disposition pitched an old stove downstairs. He remained in bed. When one of the masters asked him next day if he had heard the noise, he said that he had. When the master asked further why he had not done anything, Calvin replied, "It wa'n't my stove." The looming police strike "wa'n't" his strike: the Commissioner and the Mayor should resolve it as best they could. Since he had not appointed Curtis, he felt no responsibility for him. If a strike should occur it was up to them to safeguard the city. The attempts of the Committee of Thirty-Four to get Coolidge to intervene were in vain. As events moved to their climax over that first weekend in September, the Governor left for the western part of the state. No one in Boston knew where he was. He made sure of that.

Calvin Coolidge was the product of the Republican escalator system that worked for decades in Massachusetts with great smoothness until the Depression years destroyed its mechanism. Up the escalator went the more astute and adaptable local politicians under the benevolent surveillance of Boss Murray Crane and the general staff of the Republican state committee. Typically, Coolidge rose from mayor of Northampton to become, successively, state representative, state senator, president of the Senate, lieutenant governor, and then governor. Though patricians like Henry Cabot Lodge might be scornful of his bucolicisms, his nasal Vermont accent, and his two-family house on Massasoit Street in Northampton, Coolidge meshed into the machine. After two one-year terms as governor he would be

CONTINUED ON PAGE 90

ALL PHOTOS, UPI

Woman's auxiliary: *In flowered hat and white armband (and showing a neat ankle), one lady did her bit directing traffic.*

"But here, upon this bank and shoal of time,
We'd jump the life to come." Macbeth, *I, 7.*

No man is an island, we know; and islands themselves in our time have been steadily stripped of their isolation and their integrity. In the Pacific, the great ocean of atolls and archipelagoes, long waves beat on coral reefs as they did when Melville came, and Cook, and the earliest Polynesian voyagers; but now there are jet contrails in the sky, and fallout from nuclear tests comes down impartially on palm tree and penthouse.

Of all places in the Pacific, Hawaii is the only one which has been fully integrated into the modern world. The island chain, lying just within the Tropical zone and strung out from southeast to northwest across the path of the trade winds, was annexed by the United States in 1898 and admitted to statehood in 1959. It shares with the rest of the Union all the marks of involvement in present-day American life—benefits which have been incalculable, and burdens which include the still vivid agony of Pearl Harbor. Hawaii, as much as any other part of the United States, knows what the twentieth century is about.

But not quite all of Hawaii. The westernmost inhabited island is Niihau, separated from the larger island of Kauai by a channel seventeen and a half miles wide and twenty-five hundred feet deep. Between Kauai and its arid, low-lying neighbor, Niihau, the modern era comes to an end in deep water.

Almost one hundred years ago Niihau was bought outright from the Hawaiian monarchy by a family of immigrant Scots, who settled there to raise sheep and cattle. They virtually stopped the clock in mid-nineteenth century. As Hawaii became more and more cosmopolitan, Niihau, with its few hundred inhabitants, remained the one island where native blood and native tongue ran almost pure. With the twentieth century, monarchy gave way to territory and then to state, but Niihau managed to stay practically untouched by the shifts of government. When the Islands were opened up to the tourist trade, Niihau, only one hundred and fifty miles from the busy capital of Honolulu, on Oahu, continued unknown, remote, and mysterious.

Three generations have passed since the island became private property, and though outside pressures on the owners have never been stronger, the urge to seclusion and the resistance to change persist. If any

For a century Hawaii's westernmost islan

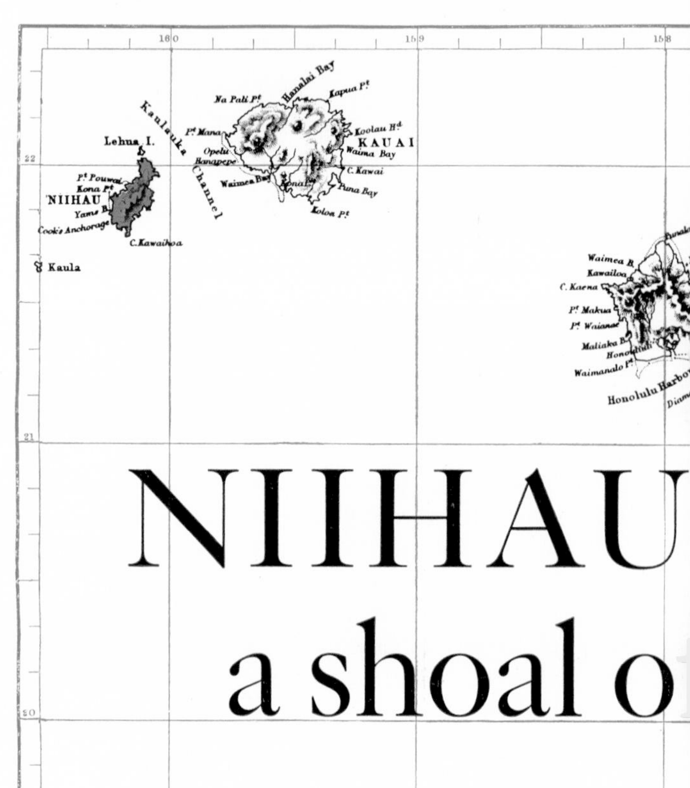

NIIHAU
a shoal o

By GAVAN DAWS AND TIMOTHY HEAD

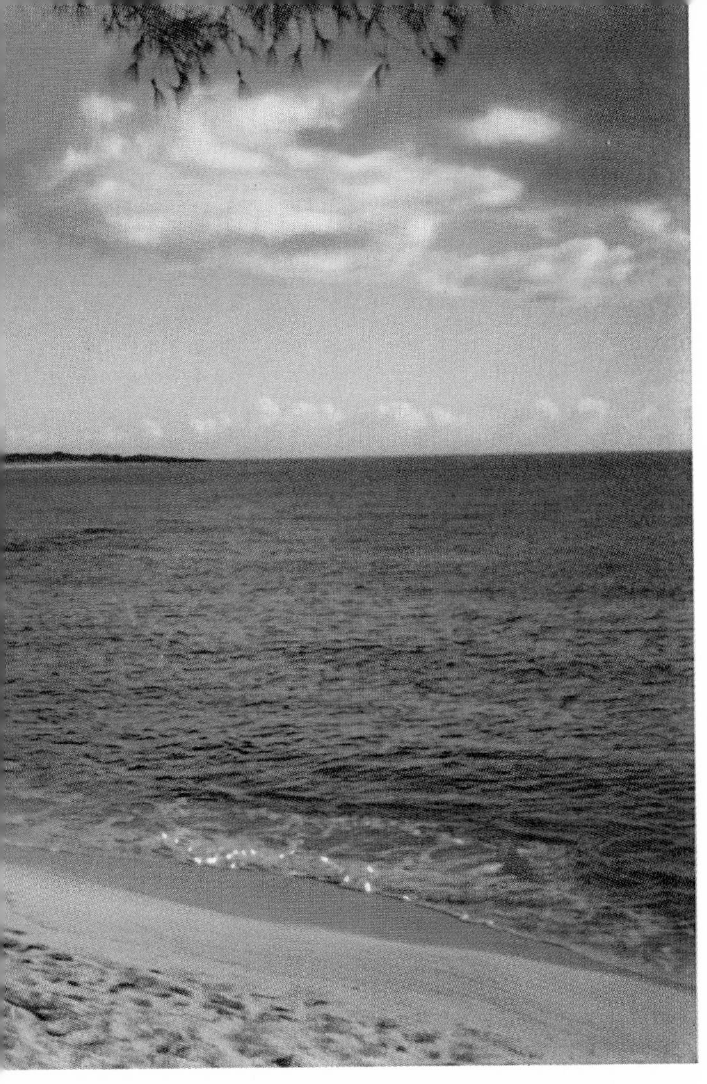

has stubbornly resisted the tides of change

ROYAL GEOGRAPHICAL SOCIETY *Journal*, 1868

time

island is inviolate, it is Niihau; if any man is an island, it is Niihau's patriarch.

Late in the eighteenth century—toward the end of the pre-white period of Hawaiian history—there were four main political divisions in the islands. Kauai formed one of these, along with Niihau, which alternated between modified independence and subjection to its more populous neighbor. Over a number of years the great warrior king Kamehameha I fought his way up the archipelago from the island of Hawaii, extinguishing independent native government as he went. He menaced Kauai in 1795–1796, but his attempts at military subjugation were unsuccessful, and unification was finally completed by diplomacy early in the nineteenth century. Over the same years white contact with the Islands had begun and was intensifying. As it happened, Niihau's experience of the outside world was never again to be so inclusive.

Oahu was the first Hawaiian island sighted by the discoverer Captain James Cook in January, 1778. Driven off from an anchorage there by winds and currents, Cook came upon Kauai and Niihau, where he spent a few days replenishing stores. The natives eagerly traded their yams and salt for pieces of iron, and relations were cordial all through Cook's brief stay. When he stood away to the north on February 1, he left behind sheep and goats and the good seed of melons, pumpkins, and onions, "being very desirous of benefitting these poor people, by furnishing them with some additional articles of food." Cook, more scrupulous than many other commanders, also made efforts to prevent his diseased sailors from infecting the natives as they had done—much to his chagrin—elsewhere in the Pacific. He had given orders that no crew members were to stay ashore overnight; but violent surf on January 30 prevented a loading party of twenty-one men from coming back to the ships, and they were not picked up until the next day. Only eleven months later Cook was in the Islands again, this time at the other end of the chain. He was mortified to find that the bad seed of venereal disease had travelled the 225 miles from Niihau to Maui ahead of him.

After Cook, Niihau's experience with white men was like that of a hundred other Pacific islands. For thirty years ships put in there more or less regularly, buying hogs, yams, and other vegetables. At least one sailor, "immoderately fond of women," jumped ship; others tried and failed. A merchant captain left three men to search for sandalwood and pearls—Niihau had neither, though Kauai had both. A convict from the British penal settlement at Botany Bay in Australia made his way to the Islands and stayed on in the service of the ruling family of Kauai and Niihau. Possibly at his instigation, a small shore party from a visiting ship was massacred on Niihau in 1796, and in reprisal buildings, canoes, and plantations were burned for a mile around the spot where the murders took place. Niihauans, by this time equipped with firearms, exchanged shots with the ship's pinnace.

A number of Niihauans left the island with departing ships—some went willingly, others were shanghaied. Two girls were kidnapped aboard the English schooner *Jenny* in the early 1790's and taken as far as Nootka Sound, where they were transferred to George Vancouver's *Discovery* and brought home via California, heavily acculturated, accustomed to shoes and stockings, and wary of showing an ankle as they went up and down the ship's ladders, but homesick for poi. Vancouver put them ashore on Kauai with a handsome gift of knives, scissors, axes, and various trinkets; and one of the two, economically most desirable, got an immediate offer of marriage from a chief.

The first Hawaiian to go to London was an adventurous Niihauan who made the trip there and back on English ships well before 1800. Almost certainly there has been no twentieth-century Niihauan who has duplicated that journey.

With the rise of the sandalwood trade and then the whaling industry early in the nineteenth century, Niihau began its long drift into obscurity. It saw only a tiny percentage of the American and European ships that came to Hawaiian ports in ever-increasing numbers. A hungry trade decimated the sandalwood stands in the uplands of Kauai and other islands down the chain, but the fragrant wood did not grow on dry, low-lying Niihau. Honolulu on Oahu and Lahaina on Maui became major whaling ports, servicing and supplying fleets on their way to and from the Central and North Pacific grounds; but Niihau, with limited resources and poor anchorages, was hardly equipped for large-scale enterprise.

Though commercially unimportant, Niihau along with Kauai attracted the attention of the Russians in the Pacific. In 1816, a Dr. Georg Anton Scheffer of the Russian-American Company, acting without approval of the Czar, negotiated an agreement with the King of Kauai, who was still restless under the suzerainty of Kamehameha I. The two islands were placed under the protection of Russia, and the Russians were given a sandalwood monopoly there. Scheffer built blockhouses on Kauai, and the King supplied him with troops to hold off any attack that might come from Kamehameha. The bubble burst in 1817, when an official Russian expedition arrived, and Scheffer, discredited, was ejected from the Islands.

With the consolidation of the Kamehameha dynasty as ruler of all the Islands, royal law was promulgated everywhere, including Niihau. Edicts from the King's court at Honolulu in the 1820's were given a strong moral tone at the urging of American Congregational missionaries, newly arrived in the Islands; and preachers stationed in outlying villages encouraged local chiefs to enforce Sabbath observance, fight drunkenness, and extirpate infanticide.

Niihau came under the jurisdiction of a Yankee missionary at Waimea, just across the channel on, Kauai, and a beginning was made in teaching the people to read and understand the Scriptures. The work was slow. Schools were set up, staffed by native teachers; but no American preacher was settled on Niihau to lead the thousand inhabitants toward the light. The Waimea pastor occasionally left his heavily populated Kauai station to make the trip across the dangerous channel, and that was all.

Twenty years passed in this way, and then Protestant concern suddenly magnified when at the beginning of the 1840's Catholicism gained a foothold, first through a native woman convert who went from Kauai to Niihau and set up a school, and then through the work of an Irish priest stationed on Kauai. In an effort to bring Niihauans back to the true God of Congregationalism, the Waimea pastor held protracted meetings on the island in 1842, and not long after that, zealous Protestants tore down a house which had been serving as a Catholic chapel.

Neither religion could claim control over Niihau. In the mid-forties the original Protestant pastor at Waimea died, and his successor reported that immediately the Niihauans "rushed again into many of their ancient vile practices and fooleries—even church members." The Catholics did no better—in 1851 their Niihau schools were disbanded for lack of competent teachers. Mormonism further confused the religious picture in the fifties, without itself becoming dominant.

With mid-century came the prospect of a basic change in the condition of the Niihauans. Like all Hawaiians, they had lived immemorially in a state approximating feudalism, owing services and payments in kind to their chiefs, and holding land solely at the pleasure of their rulers. In 1848 the Hawaiian monarchy bowed to pressure from Americans and other foreign settlers who needed clear land titles to secure their investments in the Islands, and announced the Great Mahele (division of land), a landmark in Hawaiian history which inaugurated the modern commercial era, led to the growth of the great plantations, and

PHOTOGRAPHS BY DR. MORTON E. BERK AND JACK TEEHAN

Rarely photographed, Lester (left) and Aylmer Robinson, great-grandsons of Niihau's matriarch, showed Gov. W. F. Quinn the island in 1961.

For overcoming a downed Japanese flyer in December, 1941, Benehakaka Kanahele was honored in a new song: "They Couldn't Take Niihau Nohow."

When native Niihauans—knee-high ones and big ones alike—gather before the old missionary-style church on the island, they seem to belong more to the nineteenth century than to modern Hawaii.

quickly brought Hawaii firmly into the American orbit. Under the projected reallocation of land, commoners (and in certain cases, foreigners) were able for the first time to own lots outright, subject to survey and money payment. Niihauans and others announced their readiness to buy, and eagerly petitioned the government to send them a surveyor.

Small, drought-ridden Niihau, however, produced no economic surplus to meet the cost of land, and the disappointed islanders lived out the fifties under a lease agreement with the monarchy. Even this proved burdensome, and the King's agent on Niihau complained endlessly that he could not collect the rent money. Thus Niihau's lands had not been disposed of permanently when the sixties began; but very shortly, and quite spectacularly, a buyer appeared.

On September 17, 1863, the three-hundred-ton *Bessie* anchored in Honolulu Harbor, bearing fine Merino sheep, a cow, hay and grain, chickens, jams and jellies, books and clothing, a grand piano, and thirteen members of the Sinclair family. The ship's captain was Thomas Gay, but the undisputed leader of the expedition, loved as much as she was respected, was Gay's mother-in-law. She was sixty-three-year-old Eliza McHutcheson Sinclair, widow of a Scot who had once saved the life of the Duke of Wellington by his skillful navigation.

Honolulu society heartily welcomed the newcomers, eminently respectable and wealthy as they appeared. They met Samuel Chenery Damon, the American seamen's chaplain and an influential man in the community; Bishop Staley of the Anglican Church; and Robert Crichton Wyllie, a fellow Scot and minister of foreign relations in the Hawaiian government. The Sinclairs were very receptive to Honolulu hospitality, and even more to island real-estate prospects. They were in the market for land.

A quarter-century before, Eliza Sinclair and her husband Francis had migrated from Scotland to New Zealand, where they had taken out grazing land. Now father Francis was dead, drowned on a coastal voyage, and some of the Sinclair children were married and had children of their own. As the clan multiplied, so did its land needs. Eliza's strong desire to keep her family intact meshed with her adventurous son Francis' plan for another migratory voyage. The inadequate New Zealand holdings were disposed of, and the Sinclairs sailed in their ship, the *Bessie,* for the northwest coast of America to scout territory in British Columbia.

The Sinclairs were disappointed in the Northwest, with its uncleared forest and its untamed Indians. They left Puget Sound armed with a letter of introduction from a Hudson's Bay Company man to a colleague in Hawaii; twenty-eight days later they dropped anchor in Honolulu Harbor. Chile had been on their list of possibilities—a number of New Zealand families had already settled there—but once in Hawaii they took their time, considering several potential ranch sites. The Great Mahele had dotted the land with tiny native lots, so that it was difficult for a big buyer to put together a sizable holding. But this was not the case on Niihau, where the natives had been unable to purchase. In January, 1864, two of Eliza's sons, Francis

CONTINUED ON PAGE 81

FACES FROM THE PAST–XII

The dark troubles of disunion that beset America as mid-century approached called for a man who had slain dragons (or one who appeared to have accomplished something of the sort). So the Whigs, mindful that they had won their one and only presidential election with a military man in 1840, decided to enter the lists with another in 1848. He was an authentic hero, all right: Indian fighter and frontier soldier, victor over the Mexicans at Palo Alto, at Resaca de la Palma, and—most gloriously—at Buena Vista, where he had conquered Santa Anna and a force outnumbering him four to one. What if he *had* never voted for a President? He said he *would* have voted for Clay, the Whigs' candidate, in '44, didn't he? And if he belonged to no party, what difference did that make? He held strong prejudices, and prejudices were every bit as good as principles. What was even more important from a practical standpoint, he had no personal enemies within the Whig party, as did those veteran campaigners, Henry Clay and Daniel Webster.

The electorate—drawn more readily to personalities than to ideas—conjured up its image of a man who could settle all the important problems, and decided that Zachary Taylor fitted the image. Plain, honest, uncomplicated, "Old Rough and Ready" was just about what his nickname suggests; squat and thickset, he made a better appearance on horseback than on foot because his bowed legs were so short. His face was that of a reliable farmer, burned by the Mexican sun and deeply lined by years of exposure to the elements. In Mexico his casual dress had been a source of continuing amusement to the troops: he usually wore what was handy (at Buena Vista it had been an old brown overcoat), and often appeared in a floppy straw hat and a pair of antique gray trousers. Fellow officers once estimated the total value of Zack's "uniform" at $7.50.

His appeal for the voters, based in part on deeds, stemmed also from the notion that he possessed the power to set the country right. When he did announce himself it was scarcely a resounding statement of principle: "I AM A WHIG," he proclaimed, "but not an ultra Whig." Yet that was enough to keep the voters happy; compromise, not extremes, was the order of the day. As James Russell Lowell's humorous *Biglow Papers* put it:

Another p'int thet influences the minds o' sober jedges
Is thet the Gin'ral hezn't gut tied hand an' foot with pledges;
He hezn't told ye wut he is, an' so there ain't no knowin'
But wut he may turn out to be the best there is agoin'.

When he gave an inaugural address that was one of the shortest in history, "negative and general," and poorly delivered, the crowd, ever optimistic, cheered him mightily.

In a peculiarly appropriate way, Old Rough and Ready suited the Washington of 1849. A "jumble of magnificence and squalor," it was then no more than a third- or fourth-rate town with little knots of settlement, dusty streets, and an ugly collection of brick government buildings.

The Executive mansion was of little interest to most foreign visitors, who thought it lacked splendor and taste, but Americans considered it their own, and roamed through the large public rooms almost at will, admiring the mirrored walls and flowered carpets, not to mention the President and his family. One caller at the White House left this picture of the man who was then in charge of America's destiny:

"On arriving there, I was at once ushered into the presence of General Taylor, who sat at his desk. The presidential feet rested on another chair . . . He wore a shirt that was formerly white, but which then looked like the map of Mexico after the battle of Buena Vista. It was spotted and spattered with tobacco juice. Directly behind me, as I was soon made aware, was a cuspidor, toward which the President turned the flow of tobacco juice. I was in mortal terror, but I soon saw there was no danger. With as unerring an aim as the famous spitter in Dickens's American Notes, he never missed the cuspidor once, or put my person in jeopardy."

Another visitor thought Taylor singularly unfitted by training, experience, and aptitude for the Presidency; still another said he had not one spark of genius in his soul, and that, while his purposes were honest, "the mass of his knowledge is indeed small enough." Of his Cabinet appointments, Horace Greeley wrote: "Whenever any one of them shall drop out or be 'hove over,' he will sink like a stone and never be heard of again." In all truth, there was nothing wrong with the homely virtues he possessed except their hopeless inadequacy to the job and to the times. Zachary Taylor's tragedy was that his fellow Americans confused good intentions with greatness, naïvely believing that all would be well once he was in the White House. As Francis P. Blair observed of the voters' taste in Chief Executives: "They have tried Tyler and Polk, and yet the country has not been materially hurt. If two such Presidents cannot injure the nation, nothing can!"

Only sixteen months after taking office, Taylor died (ingloriously, of too much sun, ice water, and raw fruit). And the people mourned, unaware as yet that his short term had begun a decade of unparalleled failure to find a national leader. Not until 1860 did the major parties nominate men capable of greatness. By then it was too late to save the Union.

—Richard M. Ketchum

THE PARLOR

The typical Victorian parlor: palms at the entry, a scrollwork mantel, a protective dog, and an ill-at-ease couple on not-so-easy chairs.

You entered it only rarely, and you weren't meant to be comfortable there. But every house had to have one, no matter how high the cost

By RUSSELL LYNES

To most Americans the parlor, in its stiff and overstuffed heyday, was a gesture of culture and civilization in a nation that was still more than half wilderness. It was the counterpart of the British colonial's dinner jacket in the jungle, and America was a very different sort of jungle then than now. When Sir Charles Lyell, the distinguished geologist, visited the United States in the 1840's he was moved to write, "I had sometimes thought that the national motto should be 'All work and no play.'" In some respects the parlor sought to deny this. It was a determined grab for the symbols of civilized living, and it is not surprising that in a society that was restless, ambitious, and materialistic the parlor—which represented calm, dignity, continuity, and culture—should have been set aside, its double doors firmly shut and its blinds drawn against the incursion not only of the sun but of the hurly-burly of daily life.

The parlor was not just a room in the house, but a room in a world apart, a reminder that life was not entirely made up of slop jars and broad axes, counting rooms and street hawkers. In the country and city alike it was a sort of island filled with treasure to which one could retreat on very special occasions for refreshment. It was a sanctuary of family memories, treasures brought back from travels, precious objects preserved by forebears, presents from lost friends, mementos of anniversaries, the record—in the family Bible—of the dead and the quick. Down upon all this, ancestors stared sternly out of gilt frames. To all intents and purposes the parlor was a reflection of America's determination to achieve "the good life."

But, though no room in the American home in the nineteenth century was more tenderly cared for, fussed over, or jealously protected, no room came in for more abuse and criticism. It was at once the highly polished apple of the housewife's eye, the butt of rude jokes, the pride of the family, and the target of the architect and the domestic reformer. It was the upholsterer's and decorator's gold mine, and, by the same token, the bottomless pit of the family budget. It set husband against wife, daughter against father, and swain against maiden. It was a chamber of horrors for restless children, a rack of boredom for tired men, a family chapel for the sanctification of the household lares and penates.

The parlor, a room in which to have conversation, not only derived etymologically from the French verb *parler,* but took its airs and graces from what was called in the early part of the last century "the French taste." In polite urban circles anything French was considered more fashionable than anything English, and it was not until late in the century, when the word "parlor" had become the butt of ridicule and rich Americans were buying titled Englishmen as husbands for their daughters, that the British expression "drawing room" came into polite usage in America. In general the parlor meant a room set apart for formal occasions; for entertaining acquaintances, rather than intimate friends, and clergymen on their rounds of parish calls. The word was ubiquitous, and even in the log houses of the frontier, which consisted of two square cabins joined by a breezeway or dog-trot, the room in which the family entertained guests (as opposed to the "family room," where the family cooked and ate and some of it slept) was called the parlor. In it were such treasures as had survived the trek from the East . . . a strip of Brussels carpet, a few pieces of real china, and a clutch of wax flowers in a bell jar.

Fashions in the decoration of the parlor changed considerably as the century progressed, though the spirit of the room remained constant. From the columned and gently tinted simplicity and restrained elegance of the Greek Revival parlor of the 1830's and the formality of the Gothic furnishings so warmly recommended by Andrew Jackson Downing, whose word on taste in the 1840's was law, it erupted in the fifties in plush and velvet. It became a bower of fringe and needlepoint, cabbage roses and lambrequins, ottomans and little spindle chairs on which a lady might perch daintily in her crinoline and beribboned satins but on which a man hardly dared to risk his bulk. Even late in the century, when the "artistic craze" was foisted on Americans by Charles Eastlake and furniture became solid, dowelled, and "sincere," the spirit of the parlor changed scarcely at all. It remained the island of formality in a turbulent sea of family comings and goings.

The trouble with the parlor—and to a great many

TEXT CONTINUED ON PAGE 64; ILLUSTRATIONS CONTINUE ON FOLLOWING PAGES

THE CELEBRATED RIP VAN WINKLE RECLINING ROCKING CHAIR.
Makes 15 Pieces of Furniture, and can be placed in 200 positions.

The Ag

Victorian human nature abhorred a vacuum, and massive carved furniture helped fill it. Mantels were a duster's nightmare; the one above had two crystal candelabra, three lamps, and a forest of vases. But Father put his foot down. the not-so-easy chairs were replaced by

f Clutter

something he could stretch out on (left). Organs like the one at upper right—its manufacturer promised it would "pump one-half easier than any other made" —drew the family into the parlor more often. In those pre-furnace days, a stove was a strict necessity, but it had to be "artistic."

The Etiquette of Calling

The stiffness of the parlor's furnishings was as nothing compared with the rules, appallingly detailed, for conducting oneself in it. The lady at right below, for example, might not remove her hat or coat: she was making a morning call. Fortunately, there were rule-books, like Hill's Manual of Social and Business Forms *(1880). As the page at right proves, it was a heavy vade mecum of "shoulds," "musts," and "do nots."*

THE morning call should be very brief. This formal call is mainly one of ceremony, and from ten to twenty minutes is a sufficient length of time to prolong it. It should never exceed half an hour.

In making a formal call, a lady does not remove her bonnet or wraps.

Unless there be a certain evening set apart for receiving, the formal call should be made in the morning.

It is customary, according to the code of etiquette, to call all the hours of daylight morning, and after nightfall evening.

Calls may be made in the morning or in the evening. The call in the morning should not be made before 12 M., nor later than 5 P. M.

A gentleman, making a formal call in the morning, must retain his hat in his hand. He may leave umbrella and cane in the hall, but not his hat and gloves. The fact of retaining hat indicates a formal call.

WHAT SHOULD BE AVOIDED WHEN CALLING.

Do not stare around the room.

Do not take a dog or small child.

Do not linger at the dinner-hour.

Do not lay aside the bonnet at a formal call.

Do not fidget with your cane, hat or parasol.

Do not make a call of ceremony on a wet day.

Do not turn your back to one seated near you.

Do not touch the piano, unless invited to do so.

Do not handle ornaments or furniture in the room.

Do not make a display of consulting your watch.

Do not go to the room of an invalid, unless invited.

Do not remove the gloves when making a formal call.

Do not continue the call longer when conversation begins to lag.

When a gentleman accompanies a lady at a morning call (which is seldom), he assists her up the steps, rings the bell, and follows her into the reception-room. It is for the lady to determine when they should leave.

All uncouth and ungraceful positions are especially unbecoming among ladies and gentlemen in the parlor. Thus (Fig. 6), standing with the arms akimbo, sitting astride a chair, wearing the hat, and smoking in the presence of ladies, leaning back in the chair, standing with legs crossed and feet on the chairs—all those acts evince lack of polished manners.

If possible, avoid calling at the lunch or dinner hour. Among society people the most fashionable hours for calling are from 12 M. to 3 P. M. At homes where dinner or lunch is taken at noon, calls may be made from 2 to 5 P. M.

Should other callers be announced, it is well, as soon as the bustle attending the new arrival is over, to arise quietly, take leave of the hostess, bow to the visitors, and retire, without apparently doing so because of the new arrivals. This saves the hostess the trouble of entertaining two sets of callers.

FIG. 6. UNGRACEFUL POSITIONS.

No. 1. Stands with arms akimbo.
" 2. Sits with elbows on the knees.
" 3. Sits astride the chair, and wears his hat in the parlor.
" 4. Stains the wall paper by pressing against it with his hand; eats an apple alone, and stands with his legs crossed.
No. 5. Rests his foot upon the chair-cushion.
" 6. Tips back his chair, soils the wall by resting his head against it, and smokes in the presence of ladies.

Do not remain when you find the lady upon the point of going out.

Do not make the first call if you are a new-comer in the neighborhood.

Do not prolong the call if the room is crowded. It is better to call a day or two afterwards.

Do not call upon a person in reduced circumstances with a display of wealth, dress and equipage.

Do not, if a gentleman, seat yourself upon the sofa beside the hostess, or in near proximity, unless invited to do so.

Do not, if a lady, call upon a gentleman, except officially or professionally, unless he may be a confirmed invalid.

Do not open or shut doors or windows or alter the arrangement of the room.

Do not, if a gentleman, leave the hat in the hall when making merely a formal call. If the call is extended into a visit, it may then be set aside. Whether sitting or standing (Fig. 7), the hat may be gracefully held in the hand.

Do not resume your seat after having risen to go, unless for important reasons.

Do not walk around the room, examining pictures, while waiting for the hostess.

Do not introduce politics, religion or weighty topics for conversation when making calls.

Do not take a strange gentleman with you, unless positively certain that his introduction will be received with favor.

To say bright and witty things during the call of ceremony, and go so soon that the hostess will desire the caller to come again, is much the more pleasant. No topic of a political or religious character should be admitted to the conversation, nor any subject of absorbing interest likely to lead to discussion.

General Suggestions.

Calls from people living in the country are expected to be longer and less ceremonious than from those in the city.

When it has been impossible to attend a dinner or a social gathering, a call should be made soon afterwards, to express regret at the inability to be present.

A gentleman, though a stranger, may with propriety escort an unattended lady to the carriage, and afterwards return and make his farewell bow to the hostess.

Should a guest arrive to remain for some time with the friend, those who are intimate with the family should call as soon as possible, and these calls should be returned at the earliest opportunity.

Unless invited to do so, it is a violation of etiquette to draw near the fire for the purpose of warming one's self. Should you, while waiting the appearance of the hostess, have done so, you will arise upon her arrival, and then take the seat she may assign you.

FIG. 7. GENTILITY IN THE PARLOR.

The figures in the above illustration represent graceful postures to be assumed by both ladies and gentlemen in the parlor. As will be seen, whether holding hat or fan, either sitting or standing, the positions are all easy and graceful.

To assume an easy, genteel attitude, the individual must be self-possessed. To be so, attention must be given to easy flow of language, happy expression of thought, study of cultured society and the general laws of etiquette.

Duty of the Hostess.

She should greet each guest with quiet, easy grace.

She should avoid leaving the room while guests are present.

She should furnish refreshments to those callers who come a long distance to see her.

She should be aided, upon important occasions, by a gentleman, in the reception of guests.

She should avoid speaking disrespectfully of those who have previously called upon her; she should equally divide her attentions among the several callers, that none may feel slighted.

The hostess should, if not desiring to see anyone, send word that she is "engaged" when the servant first goes to the door, and not after the card has been sent up. Should she desire certain persons only to be admitted, let the servant understand the names definitely.

Parlors — Small & Grand

The middle-class parlor at left is a testimony to the Victorians' interest in musical accomplishment—now, alas, almost vanished. One can still find a piano in the parlor, and occasionally a violin or a guitar. But where, oh where, is the banjo? Gone, along with the wicker "conversation chair" in which this decorous couple are courting. **Overleaf:** *In glittering contrast to the homey clutter of the middle classes is the formal parlor of the William Astors in New York. From left in Lucius Rossi's 1875 canvas are daughter Helen, who later married F. D. R.'s half brother, James; William, grandson of John Jacob; Charlotte Augusta ("Gussie"); John Jacob IV, later lost on the* Titanic; *Mrs. Astor; and Caroline.*

CONTINUED FROM PAGE 55

serious-minded people it was a grave trouble—was that the island occupied far too large a part of the family sea and, even more deplorably, far too large a part of the budget. One might expect such extravagance of the social butterflies and fops who lived in cities. *Harper's Bazar* in the 1860's flew into a rage of indignation because so many families in New York spent a third of their incomes renting houses at fashionable addresses and had only enough money left to make a splurge in the parlor and dining room and leave the rest of the house in a state approaching squalor. But it seemed downright immoral of the farm family, not only the bulk but the backbone of the nation, to indulge in silly notions of the same sort. And yet such was too often the case.

"So far as space is concerned," wrote Sereno E. Todd, a widely read advocate of the virtues of rural living, "most people in the country should reverse the order of their parlors and their kitchens. Most farmers erect a nice and expensive house, with a costly parlor or two, and furnished with beautiful carpets, window shades, and other adjuncts of a parlor, and go look into the—almost sacred—apartment about once a week . . . What is the use of having a house without making fair and respectable use of it?" And Mr. and Mrs. Stockton, who wrote about the home in the 1870's, encompassed all American households when they asked: "Was there ever an American woman who, furnishing a house, did not first lay aside the money for the parlor? A parlor must be, even if after it come the deluge."

If the cost of furnishing the parlor was nearly always enough to take a husband's breath away, its spiritual demands were even greater. It was the showcase of gentility, and its elaborate code of manners was filled with pitfalls for the ill-bred or the unwary. It was in the parlor that the most formal moments of family life were endured—the formal call (known as a "morning" call if it took place anytime between eleven A.M. and five P.M.), the tea party, the evening reception, the dreadful ten minutes while guests gathered before the dinner party, the hushed and lugubrious conversation when a member of the family had died, the proposal of marriage. The writers of books of etiquette had advice to offer on every aspect of behavior in the parlor, every situation, every innuendo. With indignation, with humor, or with the quiet, indulgent tones of an older and wiser friend, they anticipated every possible social gaffe. There were a great many American families who looked upon their parlors as an indispensable anchor which held their households in the social stream, but who were unsure just how one should behave in them. It was at people like these that the behavior books were aimed, and there were rules, rules, rules.

Nothing was more difficult about the parlor, for instance, than the problem of how to get into it gracefully and get out of it without fumbling. Emily Post in her first etiquette book in 1922 said, "Perhaps the best instruction would be like that in learning to swim. 'Take plenty of time, don't struggle, and don't splash about!'" Nearly a century earlier Mrs. Farrar in *The Young Lady's Friend* had felt constrained to note that on entering the parlor,

> Some girls have a trick of *jiggling* their bodies, (I am obliged to coin a word in order to describe it); they shake all over, as if they were hung on spiral wires, like the geese in a Dutch toy. . . . It robs a lady of all dignity, and makes her appear trifling and insignificant. . . . It must have originated in embarrassment, and a desire to do something, without knowing exactly what; and being adopted by some belle, it became, at one time, a fashion in New York, and spread thence to other cities.

The problem was by no means merely a feminine one. The anonymous author of *The Ladies' Indispensible Assistant,* which also included instructions for gentlemen, took a less humorous view than either Mrs. Post or Mrs. Farrar of this critical social moment: "You leave your overcoat, cane, umbrella, &c., and if the call is of any length, your hat in the entry. A graceful bow, a pleasant smile, an easy way of paying compliments, and suiting them to each person, no lesson can teach." The author, presumably a woman, added:

> It is well to know how to enter a room, but it is much better to know when and how to leave it. Don't stand hammering and fumbling, and saying "Well, I guess I must be going." When you are ready, go at once. It is very easy to say, "Miss Susan, your company is so agreeable, that I am staying longer than I intended, but I hope to have the pleasure of seeing you again soon; I wish you a good morning," and bowing, smiling, shaking hands, if the hand be proffered, you leave the room, if possible without turning your back; you bow again at the front door, and if any eyes are following you, you still turn and raise your hat in the street.

Hundreds of thousands of words were written about proper parlor conversation. The books outlined dialogue for brief, fifteen-minute calls, which consisted merely of exchanging compliments, and listed suitable topics for longer interchanges. They also indicated those topics considered socially taboo. To engage in an argument was, of course, the very nadir of taste and breeding, though the argument might be about

CONTINUED ON PAGE 96

PICTURE CREDITS: PAGE 54, NEW-YORK HISTORICAL SOCIETY; PAGES 56–57, PHOTOGRAPH BY ALICE AUSTEN, STATEN ISLAND HISTORICAL SOCIETY, ALL OTHERS, WARSHAW COLLECTION OF BUSINESS AMERICANA; PAGE 58, *Demarest's Monthly Magazine,* CULVER PICTURES; PAGES 60–61, CULVER PICTURES; PAGES 62–63, COLLECTION OF MRS. VINCENT ASTOR, COURTESY *Life.*

"In the name of the Great Jehovah and the Continental Congress!"

So bellowed Ethan Allen as he took Fort Ticonderoga without a shot. Once again the brawling giant of the Green Mountains had lived up to a myth that was indeed mighty—but no greater, perhaps, than the actual man

By KENNETH S. DAVIS

ETHAN ALLEN SURPRISING FORT TICONDEROGA

He was such a man as legend is made of—and when first we see him, in Bennington's Catamount Tavern on the evening of May 1, 1775, his gaudy legend is already so thick and close around him that we can only imperfectly distinguish it from the man himself. Must we do so in order to know him as he "really" was? After all, his legend was no imposed creation of professional image-makers. It emanated from him directly, naturally, for the most part spontaneously—though he was not above adding to it now and then by playing a quite conscious role. In all probability, the legend illuminates more of his essential character than it distorts.

For instance, as he sits now in Landlord Stephen Fay's taproom he is tossing down his huge gullet a concoction known as a "Stonewall." It consists of the hardest possible cider liberally laced with rum—a liquid hellfire of a drink—and has derived its name from the fact that it facilitates the building of those hundreds of miles of wall which every year are extended across the settled areas of New England. Not a man on the New Hampshire Grants can down more Stonewalls at a sitting than Ethan Allen.

On one occasion in this very taproom—so the story went—he drank a number unusual even for him before beginning a long journey afoot through the wilderness with his great friend and cousin, Remember Baker. When the drinks began to wear off, the two lay down beside a sun-warmed rock and fell into deep sleep. Some time later, Baker was awakened by an ominous, dry, hissing sound. Turning his head, he saw to his horror a huge rattlesnake coiled on Allen's chest, striking again and again at the arms, the shoulders, and the neck of the still sleeping giant. Springing to his feet and grabbing his gun, Baker moved cautiously to prod the snake away. Before he could do so, however, the snake slithered onto the grass, its lifted head weaving, its body fantastically writhing. Utterly astounded, Baker saw that the snake was looking at him cross-eyed! Then, incredibly, it emitted a mighty hiccup and hiccuped again as it disappeared into a blueberry thicket. Baker was still staring in frozen astonishment when Ethan Allen awoke and began to curse the "damnable blood-sucking mosquitoes" that had bitten him in his sleep. . . .

Witness, too, the sign under which Allen drinks on this May evening. It is no ordinary tavern sign. Mounted on a twenty-five-foot pole in the yard, it consists of a huge stuffed catamount with bared fangs snarling toward New York, symbolizing the "war" that has been waged by the Green Mountain Boys against the hated Yorkers these five years past. It may also remind onlookers of another often-repeated story. As Allen strode along a mountain path one day, he was attacked by the largest catamount imaginable. The great cat leaped without warning upon his back, whereupon Ethan calmly reached up over his head, grabbed his attacker by the throat, threw it on the ground before him, and strangled it to death without once relaxing his grip! When he arrived at his destination that evening he complained that the "goddamn Yorkers" had "trained . . . varmints" to claw him down. On yet another occasion, attacked by a wounded bear, he is reputed to have killed it by ramming his powder horn down its throat.

No doubt about it, this Ethan Allen is the original rough, tough, ring-tailed terror of the mountains, a giant in stature (he stands six-and-a-half feet tall), beautifully proportioned, and immensely strong. He chews up nails and spits them out as buckshot. He seizes bushel bags of salt with his teeth and throws them over his head as fast as two men can bring them to him. Alone in the woods, he encounters two surveyors for New York land claimants; lifting one in each hand, he beats them together until they yell for mercy and promise never again to set foot on the New Hampshire Grants. Alone again, he encounters a New York sheriff with no fewer than six armed deputies, all sent from Albany for the express purpose of arresting him; he lays them all senseless and bleeding on the ground without even getting his wind up.

Nor is his fighting prowess limited to physical encounters. In the war of words he is, if anything, even more effective. Take, for example, his extended comments on the Act of Outlawry passed in 1774 by the legislative assembly of New York. Governor William Tryon in Albany has been empowered to issue a proclamation commanding Ethan Allen and seven others, all named in the act, to surrender to New York authorities within seventy days or be judged "attainted of felony" and, upon capture, to suffer death without trial or benefit of clergy. This law, cries Ethan in print, is "replete with malicious turpitude!" He goes on:

> And inasmuch as the malignity of their disposition towards us, hath flamed to an immeasurable and murderous degree, they have, in their new fangled laws, . . . so calculated them, as to correspond with the depravedness of their minds and morals;—in them laws, they have exhibited their genuine pictures. The emblems of their insatiable, avaricious, overbearing, inhuman, barbarous and blood guiltiness of disposition and intention is therein pourtrayed in that transparent immagery of themselves, which cannot fail to be a blot, and an infamous reproach to them, to posterity.

And what is this quarrel with New York in which Ethan Allen has made his fame? It is a complex and involved dispute over real estate. New Hampshire, once a part of the Massachusetts Bay Colony, assumed that its western boundary was a northward extension of Massachusetts' western line—a line running some twenty miles east of the Hudson and through Lake Champlain into Canada. Its Royal governor, Benning Wentworth, felt he was sustained in this view by the fact that the first land grants in this area had been made by the provincial government of Massachusetts. He therefore ordered surveys and by 1762 had granted some sixty townships, including Bennington, which was named for him, receiving for each of them £20 in cash plus five hundred of the choicest acres reserved as his personal property. Onto these New Hampshire Grants, as the territory came to be called, settlers began to move in significant numbers after the French and Indian War. They had paid for their land; they had secured titles to it under the Crown.

The validity of these titles, however, was challenged by the provincial government of New York. The Royal governor in Albany claimed that on the basis of the original charter granted by Charles II to the Duke of York in 1664 his province extended eastward to the Connecticut River. Moreover, he managed to obtain a ruling to that effect from the Crown. He then divided the disputed territory, or the map of it, into four counties, established (on paper) a court of justice in each, and ordered the settlers to surrender their land titles and repurchase them under grants from New York. If they failed to do so their grants would be sold to New York landlords at prices of from £200 to £250 per township; the money would go into his own pocket, of course.

Naturally those who held New Hampshire titles were outraged. Very few of them complied with the Albany order. The rest promptly found themselves faced with writs of ejection issued in favor of New York landlords and backed by New York courts. They organized. They sent an emissary to the King, who, sympathizing with settlers who had already paid once for land that had since been improved by their labor, ordered New York to make no more grants pending a further study of the matter—an order New York failed to heed. Thus, as Ethan Allen explained: "[T]he inhabitants . . . [were] drove to the extremity of either quitting their possessions or resisting the Sheriff and his posse. In this state of desperacy, they put on fortitude and chose the latter expedient." Thus the legal dispute became a violent quarrel, exacerbated by the great differences in historical background and social organization between New York and New England: New York with its system of vast landholdings, its rigid class distinctions, its Tory politics; New England with its Puritan tradition, its predominance of small farmers and entrepreneurs, its relatively democratic society and growing passion for independence from George III's England.

In Bennington and Rutland counties a convention was formed whose elected delegates ruled that no person in the district could take grants or have them confirmed under the government of New York, forbade inhabitants to hold any office or accept any honor or profit from New York, and required all military and civil officers who acted under the authority of New York to suspend their functions. To enforce these rules and to defend the settlers, a military association was formed, the Green Mountain Boys, a "regiment" of some five "companies" whose colonel commandant was —and on this May evening in 1775 still is—Ethan Allen.

He it is who, with his Boys, has "seized their [*i.e.*, the New York] magistrates and emissaries, and in fine, all those their abettors who dared to venture upon the contested lands, and chastised them with the whips of the wilderness, the growth of the land they coveted." (One Benjamin Hough, who had accepted a New York

THE GREEN MOUNTAIN BOYS IN COUNCIL

commission as justice of the peace, received two hundred lashes across his naked back before being banished.) He it is who locked two captured Yorker sheriffs in separate rooms on the same side of a house one night, strung up a realistically stuffed straw man from a tree where both could see it in the morning, and then told each that the other had been hanged and that the same fate awaited him if ever he returned. (They were released to flee in separate terror to Albany, where, with an astonished mingling of relief and humiliation, they met each other on the street.)

But it is a larger quarrel than the one with New York that agitates Ethan Allen's mind as he sits this night in Catamount's dimly lit taproom. . . .

Just twelve days have passed since the bloody events of April 19, 1775, on Lexington Common and at Concord Bridge—and Ethan has assessed their significance.

Years later, describing the feelings which now animate him, he would write: "Ever since I arrived to a state of manhood, I have felt a sincere passion for liberty. The history of nations doomed to perpetual slavery, in consequence of yielding up to tyrants their natural born liberties, I read with a sort of philosophical horror; so that the first systematical and bloody attempt at Lexington, to enslave America, thoroughly electrified my mind, and fully determined me to take part with my country."

And indeed the part he has already determined to take at the earliest possible moment is as dangerously dramatic as it is politically and militarily important. What he contemplates amidst the cheerful fumes and potent furies of the guzzled Stonewalls is nothing less than the capture with his Green Mountain Boys of the most famous British strongpoint in North America —Fort Ticonderoga, situated on the western shore of Lake Champlain at a point commanding the short portage between Champlain and Lake George. Originally a French fort called Carillon, it was completed in 1755, its basic design being that originated by the brilliant French military engineer, the Marquis de Vauban. Built of stone, it has a star-shaped outer wall whose approaches were originally ingeniously prepared for defense and, within the wall, numerous bombproof shelters and firing points so arranged as to be mutually reinforcing. It gained world fame during the French and Indian War when Montcalm held it with 3,600 troops against a well-equipped but poorly led attacking force of 15,000 British and Americans; Montcalm on that occasion inflicted 2,000 casualties while suffering only 300 of his own. Even though Ticonderoga was later captured by Lord Jeffery Amherst, it is still widely regarded as impregnable—the "Gibraltar of America," as some have called it.

Ethan Allen knows better, for the British, who obtained permanent possession of the fort at the Peace of Paris in 1763, have permitted it to fall into disrepair; it is now occupied by no more than a token force. But he also knows that Ticonderoga and its neighboring fort at Crown Point may well become impregnable when they are repaired and fully manned, as they will surely be very soon. Ticonderoga can then become a springboard for British attacks southward into the very heart of the colonies, aimed at splitting them apart.

Thus Allen has resolved to capture these forts—and for the last two months plans have been pressed forward. The venture can succeed, however, only if complete tactical surprise is achieved. Secrecy must enshroud the fact that an attack is so much as contemplated, and this secrecy must extend not only to the British but also to many leading Americans who continue to hope that ultimately, in spite of everything, a nonviolent solution of the crisis will be reached. Once Allen's plan is carried out, their hope will be destroyed completely. A politically decisive act—for even in Boston no direct attack on Crown property has yet been made by the Americans—it will make the Revolution irrevocable. It may also be an act of decisive military importance: if it succeeds, it will not only deprive the British of an immense strategic advantage in a crucial area during the crucial opening months of conflict, but may also supply the rebels with war matériel they desperately need—matériel in the absence of which they cannot possibly win the battles that must be fought around and in and for the key city of Boston.

The vital path that has led Ethan Allen to the Catamount Tavern, on the eve of his rendezvous with destiny, began in Litchfield, Connecticut, where he was born on January 21, 1738, the first child of Joseph and Mary Baker Allen. A few months later his parents moved with him from Litchfield to nearby Cornwall, on the banks of the Housatonic—a raw new community hewn out of hilly, rocky, wooded wilderness, isolated, lacking even a mill. The move was natural for the family: the Allens had been a pioneering race—restless, boldly adventurous, physically and mentally independent, seeking the farthest frontier as if by instinct—ever since the first of them landed in Massachusetts in 1632. This first Allen had shortly thereafter removed with the radical Reverend Thomas Hooker, pastor of the Dorchester Company, into the wild lower valley of the Connecticut River, away from the rigorously enforced pieties of the Massachusetts theocracy. In the century since, four generations of Allens (averaging ten children per generation) had lived in eight different localities, each more newly settled than the last.

On the produce and terrific labor of a pioneer farm —carving fields out of dense woods and clearing glacial rock from them—the boy Ethan grew remarkably big and strong, wise in the ways of the woods, skilled in the handling of tools and weapons, able to follow a faint trail through the wilderness and live off the land through which he passed. He was also intellectually precocious. He had little opportunity for formal schooling. He was, as he later confessed, "deficient in education and had to acquire the knowledge of grammar and language, as well as the art of reasoning, principally from a studious application to it, which after all, I am sensible, lays me under disadvantages, particularly in matters of composition. . . ." But he was driven by a rare hunger to know and understand the things expressed in language, by a passion for speculative thought about origins and meanings, and by a poetic need to speak his piece, not just in ways understandable but in ways eloquent, moving, memorable.

Books were not easily come by in Cornwall. The Bible was the only one readily available, and he learned it well—especially the Old Testament, whose people and stories harmonized better with his immediate environment than did those of the New. He read everything else he could get his hands on, too, and asked eager questions of the best educated and most mentally alert of all those he met. Further, as he later said, he formed the habit of committing "to manuscript such sentiments or arguments as appeared most consonant to reason, lest through the debility of memory, my improvement should have been less gradual." He practiced this "method of scribbling . . . for many years, from which I experienced great advantages in the progression of learning and knowledge."

Two men chiefly stimulated and guided the growth of his mind and character. One was Joseph Allen, his father, an honorable and hardworking man who thought for himself in religious and political matters and loved to argue; despite his espousal of religious views that in the opinion of most of his neighbors were dangerously heretical, he was elected a selectman and moderator of the town meeting. Joseph Allen instilled into his eldest son's character, by precept and example, the strength of his own moral principle, but at the same time he kept the boy's mind open and flexible. He obviously recognized, too, Ethan's intellectual superiority, for he sent him to study, in preparation for entrance into Yale, under the Reverend Jonathan Lee in nearby Salisbury.

Unfortunately, the arrangement had barely begun to work when Joseph Allen suddenly died, and Ethan found himself the responsible head of a large and far from affluent family. Yale was, thereafter, an impossibility for him.

He farmed for a time. In the summer of 1757 he enlisted with other men from Cornwall in a company that marched north to Lake George, intending to help defend Fort William Henry, at the head of the Hudson River valley, from the French and their Indian allies; but the fort had been taken before the lake was reached and so the men marched back home again. These two bloodless weeks were Ethan's sole service in the French and Indian War.

During the next four years, in ways doubtless honorable but unrecorded in history, he managed to accumulate a little capital with which he and one of his cousins purchased the fifty-acre Cream Hill farm in Cornwall. He also invested in a low-grade iron ore operation near Salisbury and in a blast furnace for smelting, enterprises in which he himself both labored and supervised the labor of others. In June of 1762 he married Mary Bronson, daughter of a miller who had ground his grain from the Cornwall farm. She is a woman of whom almost nothing is now known save that she was sickly and pious and illiterate; that she was shamefully neglected by her husband though she bore him several children, three of whom (all daughters) survived him; that she nagged him unmercifully when he was at home (he seldom was); and that she died of consumption before she was fifty.

Ethan brought his bride to Salisbury, to live near his smelting enterprise. And it was in that village and at about this time that he became intimately acquainted with the second of the two men who chiefly influenced him—Dr. Thomas Young, only five years older than he, a graduate of Yale who practiced medicine in and around Salisbury. Doctor Young was a man of advanced ideas on all matters, including medicine. He once "ingrafted" (inoculated) Ethan with smallpox pus, at Ethan's request but in violation of a local ordinance against such interference with the ways of a wrathful God. Though Ethan escaped smallpox, he was threatened with prosecution; he promptly flew into so profane a rage against the two selectmen who accused him (one was his former tutor, Jonathan Lee) that he was brought into court on a charge of blasphemy and disturbance of the peace. Smallpox virus was, however, the least important of the doctor's in-

ALLEN DISPOSSESSING NEW YORK SETTLERS

oculations of the young giant who became, very soon, his disciple as well as his friend.

For Doctor Young was a deist in religion, a skeptical materialist in philosophy, and a champion of the most extreme forms of natural-rights doctrine in political theory. He loaned Ethan his books and his notes on books he had read, and he explored with the younger man the evident absurdities and self-contradictions of the orthodox Calvinist religion. One result was a release from all inhibitions of Ethan's natural propensity and talent for violent, picturesque profanity. Another was his ambition to write a philosophical work that would free the world of the stultifying myths of Christianity and substitute for them a "System of Natural Religion" based on scientific observation and the strictest logical reasoning. As a matter of fact, he and Young arranged to collaborate on this project, the survivor to publish it if the other died before the treatise was completed; both of them would work at it off and on for years.

Yet another effect of Young on Ethan was to introduce the latter to the legalistic and intellectual aspects of the then-rising conflict between New York and New Hampshire—a controversy of vital concern to the people of Salisbury, many of whom held New Hampshire land titles. Young wrote a pamphlet on the subject wherein, to Ethan's great edification, "Liberty and Property" were deemed the twin "household gods of Englishmen," so closely joined as to be inseparable.

Ethan felt himself increasingly cramped in Connecticut. For one thing, he was in rather frequent trouble with the law as a result of his swearing, drinking, and brawling. In the spring of 1765, having sold his interest in the blast furnace to one George Caldwell, he celebrated the deal by getting drunk with Caldwell and ended by fighting with him. Allen was brought before the justice of the peace on the charge that he "did in a tumultuous and offensive manner with threatening words and angry looks strip himself even to his naked body and with force and arms without law or right did assault and actually strike the person of George Caldwell of Salisbury in the presence and to the disturbance of many of His Majesty's good subjects." He was fined ten shillings.

A little later he had another violent row with Caldwell and the latter's friend Robert Branthwaite, during which he struck Branthwaite and then "in an angry and violent manner stripped off his cloaths to his naked body and with a club struck . . . Caldwell on the head," according to the official charge made by the constable who arrested all three. Hours later he again "stripped off his cloaths to his naked body and in a threatening manner with his fist lifted up repeated . . . three times [to Caldwell]: 'You lie you dog' and also did with a loud voice say that he would spill the blood of any that opposed him."

All this happened on the day before his departure for Northampton, Massachusetts, to oversee a lead mine in which he was financially interested. He moved his family with him, but his stay in Northampton was brief. The selectmen ordered him to leave after the local minister had complained of his loud, persistent, fearsome profanity.

He returned to Salisbury in disgust, and there he was soon actively enlisted in the dispute centered on the New Hampshire Grants—enlisted on the side of the Connecticut men whose titles had been first granted by Benning Wentworth. Salisbury may have become too civilized by then for Ethan's taste, but it was still a new and raw pioneering community which attached to his drunken brawling no such opprobrium as had been his lot in staid and settled Northampton. Indeed, this propensity of his may actually have recommended him, in a way, to the holders of contested titles. He was rough and tough; but such a man was needed to serve their interests in the north. He was also, they clearly realized, highly intelligent and essentially trustworthy, else they would not have entrusted him with the management of their defense in an Albany law court in the summer of 1770. The test case involved one John Small, who had received a New York grant to land in the town of Shaftsbury, and Josiah Carpenter, who had a New Hampshire title to the same land. Carpenter lost, of course (the presiding judge, Robert Livingston, was himself one of the largest holders of New York titles to the disputed land). "War" was then begun. . . .

The land grants issue gave Ethan Allen his opportunity. Here was space enough, freedom enough for a giant's full self-expression.

ith three of his brothers—Ira, Heman, and Zimri—and his cousin Remember Baker, he became a partner in the so-called Onion River Company, a loosely organized speculative enterprise which purchased some 77,000 acres along Lake Champlain north and south of the mouth of the Onion River (later renamed the Winooski). Ira operated as the principal business manager, stationed at Onion River; Heman as the Connecticut representative, in Salisbury; and Ethan as salesman, promotion man, and political lobbyist (the cost of printing his political pamphlets was charged to the company). Ethan was also the company's chief armed guard, having built two forts on Onion River land and several times driven off "trespassers"—New York titleholders—with parties of Green Mountain Boys. Thus no one on the Grants had now a greater material interest in the defeat of New York's claims—for none stood to make a greater money profit from it—than Ethan Allen.

But the essential motivation for his public activities was not economic, and no one who knew him really well ever assumed that it was. Indeed the Onion River Company had been Ira's idea originally; he had had to talk his oldest brother into it. In essence, Ethan was the very opposite of acquisitive. He may consciously have longed for a kind of mystically undefined Glory and perhaps, though this is less certain, for a coercive Power over other men; but he was no coldly calculating machine that must run wholly on energies supplied from the outside. On the contrary, he was himself an energy that must spend itself—an electric energy that radiated an aura felt by all those around him on the Grants; it entered into them, inspired them, became a means of communication between them—became, so to speak, the vital substance and texture of human community.

His sense of justice was acute. Once he visited with his Boys the town of Durham, whose residents held their titles from New York. With a little violence and many threats, he forced them to give up the New York titles and agree to buy New Hampshire ones. But when he found out a little later that the sellers of the New Hampshire titles were asking outrageous prices—as outrageous as those of the "thieving Yorker land-jobbers"—he was furious. In an open letter he told the Durham men that they "in justice ought to have [the titles] at a reasonable rate, as new lands were valued at the time you purchased them." If the New Hampshire title-holders demanded "an exorbitant price . . ., we scorn it, and will assist you in mobbing such avaricious persons, for we mean to use force against oppression, and that only."

He had a distaste amounting to loathing for all that was devious, dishonest, and underhanded in personal relationships. On one occasion a note for $150 which he had signed fell due at a time when he could not conveniently pay it. He asked for an extension, but was refused. The matter was taken into court, where Allen's lawyer sought to gain the needed time by denying that the signature on the note was genuine. Allen, sitting in a far corner of the room, listened in astonishment, then sprang to his feet and cried to his lawyer: "I didn't hire you to come here and lie! That's a true note. I signed it. I'll pay it. . . . What I employed you for was to get this business put over to the next court—not come here and lie and juggle about it!" The postponement was granted. . . .

And indeed as he slept into the dark morning hours of May 2, 1775, he had just given a further proof that selfish economic motives were subordinate in him to other, disinterested ones. When the news from Lexington and Concord first reached the Grants, many who lived there were in a quandary. They had by that time reason to believe that the Crown was on their side in the quarrel with New York and would ultimately uphold their land claims if the colonies remained colonial. The Crown would certainly do so if, at this critical juncture, they declared their loyalty to it. On the other hand, if they declared for independence and Britain won the war that must follow, New York's claims would as certainly be upheld. Hence there was at once an anxious policy meeting at Bennington—first gathered in Landlord Fay's Catamount taproom, no doubt, but soon adjourned to the meetinghouse—attended by the leaders of the Green Mountain Boys, the Council of Safety, and other principal inhabitants. At this meeting, some urged the economic advantages of adhering to the Crown. Others counselled a policy of wait-and-see. Both of these groups had in mind and doubtless stressed, some of them on the basis of bitter experience, the vulnerability of the Grants to attacks by British troops with Indian allies coming down Lake Champlain from Canada.

ALLEN HELD IN A BRITISH PRISON SHIP

But Ethan Allen scorned such prudent considerations. Since "futurity," as he called it, was "unfathomable," such decisions as faced them now must be made in terms of right versus wrong, of freedom versus tyranny. He called for bold, forthright action on the side of colonial independence—and the majority was with him. . . .

Soon after daylight on May 2, 1775, Heman Allen

dismounted from a winded horse in the yard of the Catamount, having ridden hard through the night from Pittsfield. He brought exciting news, and just the news that brother Ethan wanted most to hear.

The Revolutionary Committee of Correspondence in Hartford, which Allen had asked for help, wanted Ticonderoga taken *at once*. To finance the expedition £300 had been drawn from the Connecticut Colony treasury; Noah Phelps and Bernard Romans were on their way with it, using part of it to obtain men and supplies as they proceeded. Connecticut men had been and were being recruited, and so were men from Massachusetts; they would arrive in Bennington within a day or two to join with the Green Mountain Boys. A couple of representatives were being dispatched to Albany to consult with the leading independence man there, Dr. Joseph Young, and "ascertain" from him "the temper of the people." It was assumed that Ethan Allen, colonel commandant of the Green Mountain Boys, would lead the expedition.

Fourteen Connecticut men, including Phelps and Romans with the money, and Ethan's brother Levi, arrived in Bennington on Wednesday, May 3; they were led by Captain Edward Mott of Hartford. On the following day Colonel James Easton of Pittsfield arrived with thirty-nine men he had raised. Meanwhile Ethan had sent out calls to his Boys, asking them to assemble at Shoreham, near the southeastern end of Champlain and almost directly opposite Ticonderoga; they were to take all necessary precautions on the way to insure that word of the impending action did not reach the enemy. Anyone found on the road leading from Ticonderoga was to be seized and interrogated by Green Mountain Boys; anyone found moving toward Ticonderoga was to be forced to turn back.

On Monday morning, May 8, Ethan and the others arrived at Castleton, some twenty miles south of the final rendezvous point, Hand's Cove in Shoreham. The nerve center for the enterprise became, for the moment, Richard Bentley's house, where the leaders met to give the expedition, for the first time, a definite if loose organization. A war committee was established for overall planning and direction of the enterprise. Captain Mott was elected chairman. Ethan Allen was named to command the actual assault. This was in accordance with the promise to the Mountain Boys that they would serve under officers of their choice; Ethan was always their unanimous choice. Seth Warner, habitually Ethan's second-in-command, was continued in that post.

From Castleton, Ethan dispatched a messenger to tell all the Boys he could find in the countryside to assemble at the Cove at the earliest possible moment for an impending great "wolf hunt." This messenger was one Gershom Beach, a blacksmith whose name might now eclipse Paul Revere's if Longfellow had been a Vermonter—for Beach, according to the generally accepted story, travelled *on foot* from Castleton through Rutland, Pittsford, Brandon, Leicester, Salisbury, Middlebury, and Whitting to Shoreham, a total of some sixty miles, in just twenty-four hours!

At Castleton, Ethan also made arrangements for military intelligence. Noah Phelps was to enter the fort as a spy: he went in the guise of a farmer seeking a barber and actually did obtain a haircut. Phelps returned on the eve of the attack to tell Allen that no more than fifty troops were in the place, that they were entirely without suspicion of the impending attack, and that there was a gap, which he precisely located, in the fort's south wall. There was every chance, said Phelps, that a surprise attack would succeed.

Meanwhile the war committee had taken steps to solve the most pressing immediate problem, that of obtaining boats in which to transport the attacking force across the lake. A fifteen-year-old Castleton boy named Noah Lee had come forward with a suggestion. There were boats and even a schooner at the landing of Tory Philip Skene's nearby baronial estate, Skenesboro. Why not capture them, along with Skene and his retainers and family? Thirty men under Captain Sam Herrick were sent to do so, young Lee among them. Simultaneously, for double insurance, Asa Douglas was sent north on a boat-stealing expedition.

As things turned out, Douglas's activities were crucially important. He stopped sometime after nightfall on May 9 at the home of a Mr. Stone of Bridport. Two teen-aged boys, Joseph Tyler and James Wilcox, were asleep in Stone's house when Douglas's knock and talk of boats awakened them. They knew where a boat was. One of Skene's large scows was tied up at a Bridport landing that very moment, watched over by a Negro of Skene's whose love for liquor was notorious. The boys armed themselves with a jug of rum and a plausible tale about wanting the boat to take them to join a hunting party at Shoreham, went down to the landing, and were soon on their way to Hand's Cove. Douglas, a little later, managed to steal another boat for himself, a large one, and head for the Cove with it. Both boats arrived in the early morning darkness of May 10.

By that time, however, the situation at Hand's Cove had grown unexpectedly tense.

The rendezvous point was a deep hollow, a quarter of a mile wide in places, between heavily wooded hills. A considerable body of men could gather there without being observed from the opposite shore, and by midnight a considerable number—some 150—had done so. Huddled against the night's chill around shielded fires, they talked and laughed rather nervously together, checked and rechecked their firearms, and watched the dark, huge, striding figure of Ethan Allen. He was not a notably patient man; he sent again and again to the sentinels he had posted on shore to watch for the boats; and one may imagine the fearful oaths which poured from him as hours passed beyond the time he had set for the embarkation of his increasingly restless "army."

Nor was he in the slightest soothed when, around two o'clock in the morning, there appeared in his camp a very splendid martial figure, mounted and accompanied by a *valet de chambre* (the first ever seen, probably, in all the Grants). The stranger announced that he was Colonel Benedict Arnold and had come to take command of the assault! He had a handsome uniform, with scarlet coat and gold epaulettes that glinted in the light of a quarter moon. He had a document, a commission from the Committee of Safety in Cambridge, Massachusetts. He had, too, an imperious manner, the kind of egotistic effrontery that is sometimes characterized as the "habit of command" —and there is some evidence that, surprisingly, he was able to overawe Ethan Allen in that moment of acute anxiety.

But if Ethan wavered for a moment, his Boys did not, and they promptly made him realize that any yielding on his part would mean the end in failure of the whole enterprise. They would take their guns and go home if they were not permitted to serve, as they had been promised, under officers of their choice.

In the end, a compromise was reached. Quite possibly it was at this moment that one of the sentinels posted on the lakeshore rushed up to tell Ethan that, at long last, a boat was approaching, whereupon Ethan, anxious to avoid any further waste of time, permitted an ambiguous solution that would save Arnold's face and keep him quiet until the task was done. Arnold, he said, could march at his side as the assault was made. Arnold himself later claimed that he had agreed to share the command equally with Allen—an unlikely arrangement which was certainly not accepted by the Boys at the time.

The boat whose prow now nosed into the shore was the large scow stolen by Joe Tyler and Jim Wilcox at Bridport, and scarcely had it been beached when the second boat appeared, the one Asa Douglas had commandeered. Ethan Allen made a swift decision. He had 150 men, two boats, and two miles of open water to cross in a darkness that would be yielding to the gray light of dawn within an hour or so. By loading the boats to absolute capacity, he could get little more than half his men across in one trip; there was not sufficient time for two. Accordingly, he divided his forces. He left Seth Warner in command at Hand's Cove, to cross when the two boats returned, or immediately if Herrick's men should happen to show up with the boats from Skenesboro. He himself led the assault force—85 men, including Benedict Arnold—loading the boats so heavily their gunwales were awash.

The landing was made just north of a projection into the lake known as Willow Point. At once Allen lined up his men in three ranks, seeing them in silhouette against a horizon that was just beginning to pale with dawn, and made a little speech. According to his own account, he reminded them that they had been for years "a scourge and terror to arbitrary power," whose "valour has been famed abroad," but that "we must this morning either quit our pretensions

ENGLISH CROWDS VIEW ALLEN'S ARRIVAL IN IRONS

to valour, or possess ourselves of this fortress in a few minutes." He urged none of his men to go contrary to their will and asked those who would go voluntarily to "poise your firelocks." Every gun was lifted.

The column, headed by Allen with Arnold beside him, moved swiftly and silently into a road that led past a charcoal oven, a redoubt, a well, and around the eastern outer wall of the fort to the broken gate in the southern face. Through this sprang Ethan Allen, waving his sword. A British sentry, posted inside, sprang up, aimed his cocked musket pointblank at the charging giant, and pulled the trigger. There was a flash in the pan; the gun had misfired. The sentry then very sensibly fled, yelling at the top of his lungs to rouse his comrades, though this seemed unnecessary since Ethan and his men, pursuing him through an archway into the center of the fort, now emitted terrifying Indian war whoops. The sentry took refuge in a bombproof across the way while Ethan, briefly, formed his men in a hollow square.

Then, abruptly, all pretense of military discipline gave way, to the shocked outrage of Benedict Arnold. The men rushed with fearsome yells of "No Quarter" toward the barracks whence emerged at that moment a soldier with fixed bayonet. He made a thrust toward the nearest man but Ethan rushed him from the side and knocked him down with the flat of his sword, sparing his life on condition he point out the commandant's room. Toward this, up a stairway, rushed Ethan, yelling "Come out of there, you damned old rat!" and demanding with a string of oaths the fort's immediate surrender.

A bewildered half-naked officer (he was a lieutenant, the second-in-command) appeared at the head of the stairs, trousers in hand. What was this all about? he wanted to know. In whose name was this "surrender" demanded?

"In the name of the Great Jehovah and the Continental Congress!" cried Ethan Allen. He also roared that he would kill every man, woman, and child in the place if he did not obtain "immediate possession of the Fort and all the effects of George the Third."

Then the door of the commandant's room opened, and Captain William Delaplace, who had had time to don his full uniform, appeared. There being nothing else he could do, he surrendered his sword to Ethan Allen and ordered his men paraded without arms.

And then, for the conquerors of Ticonderoga, including Seth Warner's rear guard which soon arrived, there followed one of the gayest, most riotous binges in all American history. For "the Refreshment of the Fatigued Soldiary," Ethan appropriated some ninety gallons of rum from Delaplace's private stock (he gave the Captain a receipt for it, later paid by Connecticut), and soon all the Americans save the highly disapproving, very military Benedict Arnold were glowingly alcoholic. Arnold, indeed, provided the only discordant note in the otherwise joyous harmony of the occasion by reasserting his claim to command on the grounds that he had an official written commission whereas Ethan Allen did not. This caused Chairman Mott of the war committee to give Ethan a written commission. It also placed Arnold in considerably more personal danger than he had been in during the assault, for the drunken Green Mountain Boys derided him, threatened him, even took pot shots at him. His scarlet coat was such a splendid target.

Ethan himself stayed sober enough to write and dispatch several letters to official bodies announcing his triumph, but their language testifies to an uncommon exhilaration, even for him. Here, for instance, is his message to the "Massachusetts Provential Congress":

> I have to inform You with Pleasure Unfelt Before that on breake of Day on the 10th of may 1775 by the Order of the General Assembly of the Colony of Connecticut took the Fortress of Ticonderoga by Storm the soldiary was Composed of about one Hundred Green Mountain Boys and Near Fifty Veteran Soldiers from the Province of Massachusetts Bay the Latter was under the Command of Col. James Easton who behaved with Great Zeal and fortitude. Not only in Council but in the Assault the Soldiary behaved with such resisless fury that they so terrified the Kings Troops that They Durst not Fire on their Assailants and our Soldiary was Agreeably Disappointed the Soldiary behaved with uncommon ranker when they leaped into the fourt.

Two days later, Seth Warner took Crown Point without firing a shot (his captives were a sergeant, eight privates, ten women and children). A few days after that, Benedict Arnold was given command of the schooner that Herrick had captured at Skenesboro. He rechristened it the *Liberty* and set out for the northern end of the lake, where, without bloodshed, he captured a British sloop, the only warship on Champlain.

Thus, without the loss of a single life, with a casual and even comic air wholly incommensurate with the importance of the event, Ethan Allen's expedition reduced three key British strongpoints—Ticonderoga, Crown Point, and St. Johns in the north (for the latter was impotent so long as the Americans controlled the lake)—and obtained for the American cause what was, for its time and place, an immense booty: upward of a hundred cannon (the figure is uncertain), several huge mortars and two or three howitzers, 100 stands of small arms, ten tons of musket and cannon balls, three cartloads of flints, a warehouse full of boat-building materials, thirty new carriages, and sundry other war supplies. Next winter, in one of the logistical triumphs of the Revolution, General Henry Knox, on orders from Washington, transported much of the Ticonderoga matériel by sled across the snows to Cambridge; Ticonderoga cannon, at once set up on Dorchester Heights, may well have decided the battle for Boston in favor of the Americans (see "Big Guns for Washington" in the April, 1955, American Heritage).

Of at least equal and more immediate importance was the effect of Allen's feat on American morale. The British were not invincible! Plain Americans were more than a match for them. A thrill of pride, an increased self-confidence spread throughout the colonies, overcoming the vacillating timidity which at first prevented the Continental Congress from operating at all effectively as the ruling body of a country at war.

Witness the first communication Ethan Allen received from the Congress after the news of his conquest had reached it. He was ordered to remove the captured war matériel to the south end of Lake George for safekeeping until such time as it could be "returned to His Majesty" when the "former Harmony" between Great Britain and the Colonies, "so ardently wished for by the latter," was re-established! Ethan's response was explosive. He was "God damned" if he would obey such an order. "It is bad policy to fear the resentment of an enemy," he wrote back, obviously contemptuous, in a letter recommending an immediate attack on Montreal, it being his "humble [sic] opinion, that the more vigorous the Colonies push the war against the King's troops in Canada the more friends we shall find in that Country."

Subsequently he decided to go personally before the Congress in an effort to inject into this apparently flabby body some rigidity of courage and initiative. Accompanied by Seth Warner, he headed for Philadelphia by way of Bennington, arriving in the latter place (according to plausible legend) on a Sunday when the Reverend Jedediah Dewey preached a sermon of thanksgiving to God on the capture of Ticonderoga. Ethan, having been told what the sermon subject would be, attended, but grew increasingly restive as the minister in an interminable prayer thanked God over and over again, in the most abject humility, for the great fort's downfall. At last Ethan could contain himself no longer. He rose in his place, to the astonishment of the congregation, and reminded Parson Dewey in a loud voice that God had not reduced the fort without assistance. "Aren't you going to mention the fact that I was there?" he demanded. To which Parson Dewey is said to have replied: "Ethan Allen, thou great infidel, sit down and be quiet!"

In Philadelphia, Allen, as the hero of Ticonderoga, managed to inspire the Congress with some of his own optimistic courage. The raising of a regiment from the Grants, to serve under officers of its own choosing, was authorized. A proposed attempt upon Montreal was approved. But so far as his influence upon our national destiny is concerned this was perhaps the high point of Ethan Allen's career.

There followed for him a period of grave personal misfortune. To the surprise of almost everyone and to his own deep hurt, he was not chosen to command the Grants regiment, nor was he even made a subordinate officer of it. The voting was done not by active Green Mountain Boys but by a meeting of various town committees—older men who had long frowned upon Ethan's heretical views and riotous ways and who feared his impetuosity. Their choice for colonel of the regiment was the relatively staid, sober-minded Seth Warner. It is a measure of Ethan's bigness of character that in his disappointment he did not attempt to sabotage the regiment: he did all he could to insure its and Warner's success. However, there seems no doubt that the rebuffs he had received made him over-eager to perform great deeds. He was used as an advance scout and recruiting agent by General Philip Schuyler and General Richard Montgomery, who were mounting the expedition to take Canada, of which Warner and the Green Mountain Boys were also a part.

SOLITARY CONFINEMENT IN A NEW YORK MILITARY PRISON

He was without commission or authority when, one day in that autumn of 1775, he rashly attempted to take Montreal with a bare handful of men and was himself captured instead, with such of his men as had not deserted him, after a noisy if remarkably unsanguinary gun fight. His capture was the forerunner of a greater misfortune for the Americans. Though a force commanded by Montgomery managed to take Montreal, it was defeated and Montgomery killed at Quebec that December.

Allen spent the next two and a half years as a British prisoner of war—a year in England, the rest aboard ships at sea and in British-held New York City.

Upon his release in an exchange in May of 1778, he visited General Washington at Valley Forge. The latter immediately wrote to the President of the Congress about him, praising his "fortitude and firmness" which seemed "to have placed him out of the reach of misfortune." Washington went on: "There is an original something in him that commands admiration; and his long captivity and sufferings have only served to increase if possible, his enthusiastic zeal. He appears very desirous of rendering his services to the States, and of being employed; and at the same time he does not discover any ambition for high rank. Congress will herewith receive a letter from him; and I doubt not they will make such provision for him, as they may think proper and suitable."

But Ethan never actively served under the commission which the Congress gave him. His personal fame was augmented and the national interest served by his publication, in the spring of '79, of a personal narrative wherein he told of taking Ticonderoga and of his "Captivity and Treatment by the British." It was an exciting adventure story which went through eight editions in two years, and its account of his mistreatment by his captors (he had indeed been cruelly handled) was effective in fanning popular hatred of the enemy. His subsequent career, however, was identified not with the emergent United States but with the emergent state of Vermont, to whose interests, as a matter of fact, he soon sacrificed much of his reputation as national patriot.

As early as March 1, 1775, Ethan in a letter to Oliver Wolcott had boldly proposed that the Grants be transformed into a distinct and independent state—a state free alike of New York and New Hampshire. When he returned as a hero from his long captivity he found his dream becoming a reality. Shortly after Ethan's capture, General Montgomery had been killed, and the Canadian expedition had been abandoned, leaving the Grants' frontier to the north and northwest unprotected against the enemy. Rather than call for protection from the New York militia, thus tacitly admitting Yorker sovereignty over them and endangering their land titles, the men of the Grants determined to defend themselves. Early in 1777, in a convention assembled at Westminster, they declared the Grants to be a free and independent state—at first called New Connecticut—petitioning the Congress for admission to what was then known as the Association of States. (It was Ethan's old friend and mentor of Salisbury, Dr. Thomas Young, who first suggested the name Vermont—French for Green Mountain—a suggestion that had happily been accepted.) Since the Congress had thus far refused to recognize the new state's existence, even though it had established a constitution (the first in America specifically to prohibit slavery) and had elected a governor, a legislature, and other officers, Vermont considered itself to be, and Ethan certainly considered it to be, an independent republic. To it he now gave his whole allegiance; of it he promptly became, as he had been on the Grants of old, the leading man.

It was in this role that he entered upon the most dubious phase of his career. During the closing years of the Revolutionary War he secretly intrigued with the British in Canada in order to prevent an invasion of his republic from the north, at the same time roaring his defiance of every order of the Congress which did not recognize Vermont's independence or which seemed to threaten the legal title of Vermonters to the land they occupied. Such military activity as he engaged in during this period was aimed not at the British but at the suppression of "treason" within his republic and at Yorker (and congressional) threats from without. When the actual fighting of the Revolution had ended, Vermont was still an independent republic. She remained so until March 4, 1791, when, in the third session of the Congress, under the Constitution of the United States, she was admitted to the Union as the fourteenth state—an event for which Ethan Allen was more responsible than any other man.

But by the time it occurred he had been dead more than two years, and even in the state he had done so much to create, his name was under something of a cloud.

In part this was due to his British intrigues: there were many even in Vermont who looked upon these mysterious activities as treasonable. But mostly it was due to his publication in 1784 of the philosophical and religious work which he and Dr. Thomas Young, who died in 1777, had projected when they were young men together in Salisbury long before. The work's full title indicates its scope and nature: *Reason, The Only Oracle of Man; Or, A Compenduous System of Natural Religion, to which is Added Critical Remarks on the Truth and Harmony of the Four Gospels with Observations on the Instructions Given by Jesus Christ and on the Doctrines of Christianity.*

It is a work of some importance in American intellectual history, though now almost forgotten, for it helped to relax the strong hold of orthodox Calvinism on the New England mind and conscience. "As far as we understand nature, we are become acquainted with the character of God," wrote Ethan, "for the knowledge of nature is the revelation of God." He attacked the central dogma of Calvinism by arguing that "Human liberty, agency and accountability, cannot be attended with eternal consequences, either good or evil." The book was denounced and its author abused in print and from a hundred pulpits; even to own a copy was to be suspected, by the pious, of infidelism.

Consistent with the view of Ethan as an "awful Infidel, one of ye wickedest men yt ever walked this guilty globe" (so said one Reverend Nathan Perkins, who looked upon Allen's grave with "pious horror"), was the widely told and evidently true story of Ethan's second marriage. His first wife having died in Sunderland in 1783 while Ethan, typically, was not at home, he was available and vulnerable to the very real charms of a young widow named Fanny Montresor Buchanan, whom he met early in 1784. She was the stepdaughter of a notorious Tory named Crean Bush, who had committed suicide in disgrace in 1778, and the widow of a British officer killed in an early action of the Revolution. She was as widely different in all respects from poor Mary Allen as one woman may be from another.

She was beautiful, imperious, vivacious, and impious. When Allen first met her and promptly let it be known that he desired her, she was told by someone that if she married him she would "be queen of a new state." "Yes," she replied, "and if I married the Devil I would be queen of hell." But marry him she did, after a scandalously brief courtship. The ceremony was performed by Judge Moses Robinson, chief justice of the Republic of Vermont, and was shockingly interrupted by Ethan when the Judge asked him if he promised "to live with Fanny Buchanan agreeable to the laws of God." Allen refused to answer until the Judge agreed that the God referred to was the God of Nature, and the laws those "written in the great book of Nature." He then made the necessary promise and left for Sunderland with his bride a few minutes later.

A daughter and son were soon born to them, the latter in 1787 shortly after they had moved (retired, as Ethan put it) to a farm near Burlington.

It was on this farm, two years later, during one of the hardest winters in all Vermont history, that he died. The manner of his departure was of a piece with the manner of his living. He had driven with his Negro hired hand across the thick ice of Lake Champlain to South Hero Island, to borrow a load of hay from his cousin Ebenezer Allen. Ebenezer had sent out word that Ethan was coming, so there was soon assembled a large party abundantly supplied with Stonewalls and punch and flip—many of them old Green Mountain Boys—for a carouse that lasted most of the night. Shortly after daylight—and after a final stiff drink—Ethan was deposited atop the sled-load of hay and there he lay in seeming peace as the Negro drove the team homeward. On the way he suffered what the newspapers of the time called an "epileptic fit." A few hours later, on February 12, 1789, he was dead.

When news of the event reached New Haven, the Reverend Doctor Ezra Stiles, president of Yale, known as an "inveterate chronicler" of things which might interest posterity, noted in his diary: "General Ethan Allen of Vermont died and went to Hell this day."

Ethan himself, without undue seriousness, had anticipated a different otherworldly fate. He was fond of telling about a dream he had had in which he was among several men standing in line at heaven's gate. One by one the men were questioned by the gatekeeper; then each of those admitted was asked to sit in a specifically designated seat inside, there to await further disposition. Not so Ethan Allen. The gatekeeper looked at him sharply when he gave his name.

ILLUSTRATIONS FROM *Harper's Monthly*, NOVEMBER, 1858

"You're the man who took Ticonderoga?" the gatekeeper asked.

"The very same."

The gatekeeper's stern visage broke into a warm smile.

"Come in," said he. "Come in, Ethan! Sit down wherever you please!"

Kenneth S. Davis is the author of several books, the most recent of which is a biography of Charles A. Lindbergh, The Hero. *He is at present working on a history of World War II for the Doubleday "Mainstream of America" series.*

For further reading: Ethan Allen, *by Stewart H. Holbrook (Macmillan, 1940);* A Narrative of Ethan Allen's Captivity, *by Ethan Allen (Corinth Books, 1961).*

The Steamboat's Charter of Freedom CONTINUED FROM PAGE 43

trouble in the New Jersey legislature, and he proposed to be a thorn in the side of the monopoly by breaking the New York statute wherever and whenever he could.

For this latter project he had ready, in the rude but cunning person of Cornelius Vanderbilt, master of the *Bellona,* precisely the instrument he needed. Together they invented many ingenious ways of outwitting the monopoly. One of the finest of these was to run passengers in the *Bellona* out of Elizabethtown Point and transship them, in Jersey waters, to the *Nautilus* of Daniel D. Tompkins, who had acquired from the monopoly the ferry rights between Staten Island and New York. Tompkins was an old opponent of the Livingston faction in the New York Republican party and was not unwilling to make a little mischief. The physical risks of transshipment were far from negligible, but Americans were made of stern stuff in those days, the fare of fifty cents a head was undeniably attractive, and all was going beautifully—until brought to a halt by the decision of Chancellor Kent in *Ogden v. Gibbons* of December 4, 1819.

The web of litigation was already tangled. Ogden had earlier sued Gibbons—in *Ogden v. Gibbons,* October 6, 1819—on the grounds that Gibbons was running his two steamboats between New Jersey and New York, in open defiance of the monopoly rights that Ogden had purchased from Livingston, and on this occasion Gibbons had at least wrung from Kent what he most needed, a ruling upon the scope of national coasting licenses. Nobody could deny that an act of Congress of February 18, 1793, permitted vessels of over twenty tons' burden to be enrolled and licensed. The question was: Did this national license permit a vessel to trade, not only between port and port of one state, but also between a port in one state and a port in another? If it did, there would be little comfort thereafter for the Livingston-Fulton monopoly.

Chancellor Kent, however, was now ready with an ingenious reply. A national license, he said, merely conferred upon any given vessel a national character, freeing it from those burdensome duties which were imposed upon foreign vessels if they attempted to engage in the coasting trade. That it was a license to trade, still less to trade in waters restricted by a state law, he steadfastly denied. Was it likely, he asked, that the New York steamboat acts, every one of which had been written and passed subsequent to the act of Congress, would have been written and passed at all if it could have been held that the act of Congress had annihilated them all in advance?

Gibbons, of course, promptly appealed Kent's ruling to the New York Court of Errors; the appeal was heard in January, 1820. Gibbons' counsel now contended that the licensing act was derived from the eighth section of the first article of the federal Constitution—from the power of Congress, that is, to regulate commerce among the several states. Thus, in the case of *Gibbons v. Ogden* in the New York Court of Errors there dawned what was afterward to become the high nationalist noonday of *Gibbons v. Ogden* in the Supreme Court of the United States. Justice Jonas Platt, pronouncing the decision of the Court of Errors, upheld Chancellor Kent; and against this decision Gibbons appealed to the Supreme Court.

The times, if not necessarily the law, were now certainly on Gibbons' side. With the passing of the War of 1812, a new light seemed to fall upon the map of the United States. The nation, now figuratively facing westward, began to think of its lamentable roads, its lack of canals, the primitive counterclockwise motion of its exchange of staples for manufactures as that exchange moved down the Ohio and the Mississippi on rafts and flatboats, up the Atlantic coast, and back across the Appalachians. That the steamboat might do much to reverse this process, nobody now doubted: but the steamboat, a strange but sufficient symbol of nationalism, was struggling in the grip of a monopoly dubiously bottomed upon the doctrine of states' rights.

Nor was this all. The contest between state-conferred steamboat monopolies and the clash of state retaliatory laws threatened to reduce the nation's commerce to that particularist chaos which the Constitution itself had been providentially designed to avert. And here the indefatigable Thomas Gibbons was not backward. He persuaded the New Jersey legislature to pass a new retaliatory act, and on February 20, 1820, it did so. By this act, any nonresident of New Jersey who enjoined a New Jersey citizen, in the Chancery Court of New York, from navigating by steamboat any of the waters between the "ancient" shores of New Jersey, could in turn be enjoined by the Chancery Court of New Jersey from navigating between those "ancient" shores. Moreover, and this was the sting, he could be made liable for all damages, *with triple costs,* in any action for trespass or writ of attachment which he had obtained against a New Jersey citizen in the New York court.

Thus John R. Livingston, to his dismay, discovered that his *Olive Branch* had been detained and attached in New Brunswick to answer for damages alleged to have arisen from the injunction he had won against

Gibbons in May, 1819. Threatened with successive attachments and prohibitive costs, he had at one time withdrawn the *Olive Branch* from service. In *Livingston v. D. D. Tompkins* (June 1, 1820), *Livingston v. Gibbons* (August 26, 1820), and *Livingston v. Gibbons, impleaded with Ogden* (May 8, 1821), one may trace his efforts, on behalf of Ogden as well as himself, to wriggle out of this predicament. But, alas, there was in Livingston's character just a touch of Sir Giles Overreach; he succeeded only in arousing the wrath of Chancellor Kent, a high-minded gentleman who cared little for the stratagems of entrepreneurs, but much for the dignity of the law.

Actually, Chancellor Kent had now thrown in the sponge. He had done his best for the rights and dignity of his state and his court; he might talk about state reprisals and jurisdictions until the very walls of his courtroom reverberated with his declamations; but he was, after all, one of the first jurists in the nation; and there had been growing upon his shuddering inner vision, feature by feature, like some Cheshire cat's, the implacably smiling visage of the commerce clause of the Constitution. In the meantime, he had left the quarrel between Ogden and Gibbons in a state of armed neutrality, and Gibbons and Vanderbilt continued, by one device or another, to keep the *Bellona* steaming between New Jersey and New York until such time as the Supreme Court should rule upon Gibbons' appeal from the New York Court of Errors.

This appeal had been docketed with the Supreme Court in 1820, dismissed for technical reasons in 1821, docketed again in 1822, and continued from term to term until February, 1824. By that time and in that political climate, with nationalism and states' rights opposed on many fronts, it was already a famous case. Eminent counsel had been briefed on both sides: Daniel Webster and Attorney General William Wirt for Gibbons; Thomas J. Oakley and Thomas Addis Emmet for Ogden and the monopoly.

One might have supposed, since the nationalist John Marshall was Chief Justice and the Court was supposedly "Marshall's Court," that a decision in favor of Gibbons was a foregone conclusion. But the assertion that Congress could actually regulate interstate trade was in those days a very daring one; and although John Marshall was a bold man, many people doubted if he would be as bold as all that. Nor could one be sure that, in this instance, he would be supported by a majority of his brethren.

The legal questions were extremely complicated, and Gibbons' able lawyers exploited every possible argument. Wirt, for example, reasoned that the monopoly laws conflicted with certain acts of Congress and were therefore void. Webster, however, who opened for Gibbons, went boldly to the heart of the matter by claiming that it was of no moment whether or not the New York statutes were in conflict with an act of Congress. The constitutional authority of Congress was such that it had the power exclusively to regulate commerce in all its forms upon all the navigable waters of the United States. Afterward he said—whatever Webster's faults, self-depreciation was not among them—that Marshall took in his words "as a baby takes in his mother's milk." This was not quite the case. The truth seems to be that the two men thought very much alike on the question, but that it required all Marshall's gifts to weave into a more prudent form the arguments so vehemently presented by Webster.

The pleadings consumed four and a half days, and it was generally conceded that every one of the counsel had surpassed himself—in learning, in subtlety, in eloquence. Nearly a month passed before Marshall delivered the Court's opinion. It was one of the most statesmanlike he had ever penned, and, from a legal

Gleason's Pictorial, APRIL 1, 1854

An old woodcut shows a steamboat landing at South Amboy, New Jersey. The Livingston interests contended that the monopoly bestowed by New York State gave them control of the Jersey shore of the Hudson River as well as of the New York side.

BETTMANN ARCHIVE

OLD UNION LINE,
FOR PHILADELPHIA.

Via New-Brunswick, Princeton, Trenton, & Bristol.

Fare Through, $5.

The Vice-President's Steamboat NAUTILUS will leave New-York every day (Sundays excepted) from Whitehall Wharf,

At 11 o'clock A. M.

for Staten-Island. From her the passengers will be received without delay into the superior fast sailing Steamboat BELLONA, Capt. Vanderbelt, for Brunswick; from thence in Post Chaises to Trenton, where they lodge, and arrive next morning at 10 o'clock in Philadelphia with the commodious and fast sailing Steamboat PHILADELPHIA, Capt. Jenkins, in time to take the Old Union Line Baltimore Steamboat, which leaves at 12 o'clock every day.

For seats, apply at No. 145 Broadway; No. 5 Courtlandt-st. 2d office from Broadway; at the Steamboat Hotel, corner of Washington and Marketfield-sts; at Messrs. J. & C. Seguine's, Whitehall; or Capt. De Forest, on board Steamboat Nautilus.

N. B. This line arrives in Brunswick three quarters of an hour before the Olive Branch Line.

Thomas Gibbons and Cornelius Vanderbilt, the financier who began his career as a Staten Island boatman, set up the Old Union Line to fight the Livingston steamboat monopoly.

point of view, one of his soundest. And one should always remember, as Justice Felix Frankfurter says, that when Marshall applied the commerce clause in *Gibbons v. Ogden* "he had available no fund of mature or coherent speculation regarding its implications." Like the steamboat itself, the decision which freed the steamboat was a pioneer.

Marshall began by defining "commerce" not in the strict sense of "buying and selling" (as Ogden's counsel had urged) but (this was Wirt's definition) as "intercourse," which, of course, included navigation. It comprehended also the power to prescribe rules for carrying on that intercourse.

This being the case, one had then to ask whether the power of Congress, under the commerce clause, invalidated the monopoly statutes of the state of New York. Here Marshall ruled that the coasting license act of 1793, dealing with the subject matter of that clause, was superior to a state law dealing with the same subject matter. Thus Gibbons' license did not merely confer upon his vessel an American character; it also permitted that vessel to trade between the port of one state and the port of another; nor did the fact that it was a *steamboat* have any relevance. Marshall's majestic reasoning struck down the monopoly in twenty words: "The laws of Congress, for the regulation of commerce, do not look to the principle by which vessels are moved."

Congress, in short, had power over navigation "within the limits of every State" so far as navigation may be, in any way, connected with foreign or interstate trade. (It should be remarked in passing that it took two more suits in the New York courts to determine whether or not the Livingston-Fulton monopoly was valid for purely *intra-state* commerce. Chief Justice Savage in the Court of Errors—*North River Steamboat Co. v. John R. Livingston,* February, 1825—declared that it was not.)

The subtleties, the complexities, the mass of subsequent legal glossing, the vexed questions of state taxing and state police powers—all these are irrelevant to this bare narrative: the point is that Marshall's great decision, which has been called "the emancipation proclamation of American commerce," has substantially survived the erosions of time and of change. Its immediate effect was to set the steamboat free on all the waters of the United States. Its more distant effects were beyond the scrutiny of Marshall and his contemporaries: the railroad, the telegraph, the telephone, the oil and the gas pipe-lines, the aeroplane, as they moved across state borders, all came under the protection of *Gibbons v. Ogden.*

The decision was the only popular one which Marshall ever rendered. And yet there were many dissidents. Slaveowners, for example, were deeply alarmed for the future of the interstate slave trade. Others, more selfless and high-minded—and of these Thomas Jefferson was the first and greatest—saw in *Gibbons v. Ogden* only a despotic extension of the powers of the federal government. What Gibbons and Ogden had to say has not been recorded for the instruction of posterity. One might, however, add by way of postscript that Ogden died a bankrupt and Gibbons a millionaire. Since Ogden was undoubtedly the more estimable of the two, one wonders whether the outcome proves the injudiciousness of yielding to a monopoly, or the advantage of breaking the law.

English-born but for many years an American citizen, George Dangerfield is equally at home in the history of both his native country and his adopted one. Among his books are The Strange Death of Liberal England, The Era of Good Feelings—*which carried off both the Pulitzer and Bancroft prizes—and, most recently, a biography of Robert R. Livingston.*

For further reading: Mr. Dangerfield's Chancellor Robert R. Livingston of New York 1746–1813 *(Harcourt, Brace, 1960); The* Supreme Court in United States History, *by Charles Warren (Little, Brown, 1926); and* The Life of John Marshall, *by Albert J. Beveridge (Houghton Mifflin, 1916–19).*

Niihau: a Shoal of Time

CONTINUED FROM PAGE 51

and James, acting for the clan, put a proposition to the monarchy. They would buy the island outright for $6,000. The King's cabinet council considered the offer, and made a counterproposal—$10,000 for a fee-simple title, or a lease for $750 a year. The Sinclairs elected to buy. The sale was concluded at the monarchy's price on January 23, 1864, with the warm approval of Foreign Minister Wyllie, who expressed his satisfaction at seeing people of such substance settled in Hawaii.

What had the Sinclairs bought? For just under twenty-two cents an acre, they got seventy-two square miles of land, mostly low-lying, hot and dry, sparsely wooded, and uncertainly watered. Just across the channel on Kauai, rain, trapped in high mountains, was superabundant, but the same mountains cast a rain shadow over Niihau, and natives there had to depend on small catchments and wells that yielded only brackish water. The Hawaiian staple of taro, an irrigated plant from which poi was made, would not grow; and trees were so scarce that the islanders had to barter for wood to build canoes. There were periodic temporary emigrations. Nathaniel Portlock, there in the 1780's, had traded iron for yams; and immediately many newly rich Niihauans took their western wealth to Kauai, where the living was easier. Droughts were chronic: when Vancouver had brought the two Niihau women home from their involuntary journey to the Northwest, he had put them ashore on Kauai because most of the Niihau population had gone there to escape an extended dry period.

Unsatisfactory for Hawaiian wet agriculture, Niihau offered better prospects for livestock. It had one great advantage. Elsewhere in Hawaii the ubiquitous dogs of the Polynesians were a menace to sheep and cattle; on Niihau, bounded by coast line rather than fences, this problem was quickly mastered. However, the hardy descendants of the goats left by explorers in the early days of white contact stayed on, close-cropping the grass and causing erosion until the early twentieth century, when they were finally eradicated.

Goats remained, but half of the island's population soon departed, irrevocably deprived of any hope of getting title to land on their home island. Just before the Sinclairs came, there were almost 650 Hawaiians on Niihau; two years later there were 325, and the population continued to decrease, levelling off later in the century below 200. Immediately on taking over, the Sinclairs bought out a chief who owned two parcels of Niihau land, and this left just one Hawaiian landowner on the island, a man named Papapa, who had managed to buy fifty acres when the island was thrown open for purchase during the 1850's. Papapa retained his lot for fifteen years while the Sinclairs developed their 46,000-acre holding around him. Eventually he sold to the clan, with the understanding that he could live out his life on his land.

The Sinclairs established themselves on a bluff at Kiekie overlooking a stretch of westerly coastline. Here they lived for a few years until Mrs. Sinclair, growing old, began to feel the heat of the Niihau summers. Then land was bought on the western side of Kauai, in spectacular, magnificently rich country; and there the old lady settled with most of her children around her. The Kauai ranch, called Makaweli, became the economic center of the Sinclair operations.

The style of life they developed there and on Niihau was one that fully justified for them the long migration that had brought them from Scotland to the North Pacific. They worked hard, the rewards were great, and their souls were their own—and God's. The younger generation quickly took on the tone of the congenial land around them. They learned the island language and became expert horsemen; and the men and boys learned to ride surfboards like natives.

On Niihau the Hawaiians made their own adjustments. They continued to fish and grow vegetables and to practice some of their old crafts, making mats celebrated for their soft texture and intricate weave, and stringing leis of shells peculiar to their coast line. These they sold to outsiders at good prices. For the rest, they abided by the total prohibition on liquor imposed by the dry Scots, halfheartedly sent their children to school, worshipped at the Puuwai village church with its New England steeple and native pastor, and worked for the Sinclairs, tending the stock which grazed among the ruins of old grass huts and abandoned altar sites. In at least one basic way their life had not changed much. They had merely traded an *alii* for a *haku*—a chief for a master. The classic relation between Hawaiian and white man in the nineteenth century was one of muted feudalism, in realization of the common benefits to be obtained from ready service on the one hand and good management and protection on the other; and nowhere was this better exemplified than on the Sinclair lands.

The hierarchy of authority came to a peak in the remarkable person of Eliza Sinclair, as vital as she was charming. Mrs. Sinclair was as old as the century, and she died in 1893. Control of the expanded and flourishing family estates passed to her grandson Aubrey Robinson, who had made the trip in the *Bessie* as a ten-year-old. Under his management massive irrigation works and reforestation programs were carried out at Makaweli, and both there and on Niihau he introduced many species of animals and plants in a continuing attempt to produce a diversified ecology—the first Arabian horses ever seen in Hawaii, game birds, coffee, tea, honey bees, cotton, and several new varieties of trees.

Aubrey Robinson was a well-educated and much-travelled man who had earned a law degree from Boston University and toured much of Europe and the Orient before coming back to the Islands to stay. Nothing that he saw in the outside world, however, changed his view of the family's duty toward the Niihauans. It was a stern duty, expressed in the language of a fundamental Christianity totally unaffected by the religious and social modernism of his times. Soon after Aubrey assumed leadership, Hawaii passed under American control, but the new territorial government failed to pick up responsibility for Niihau as it began to do for the rest of the Islands. As the old Hawaii faded and disappeared elsewhere, the Robinsons' will to keep Niihau unchanged grew in strength.

When it came Aubrey's turn to die in 1936, the press obituaries described him as a man who paid his debts and taxes, and as a great patron of church and missionary work. At his death the family estates were assessed as worth more than three and a half million dollars. Of this Niihau contributed only $225,000; and its economy was beginning to show signs of strain which were to become more pronounced as time went on. Clearly, strong reasons other than money guided the Robinsons in their defense of the island against the outside world.

The outside world was at that moment on the point of breaking in. As the political situation in the Pacific worsened during the thirties, military installations in Hawaii were strengthened. An Air Corps colonel visited Niihau and was disturbed to see a great amount of open country that might possibly be used as a base for a surprise air attack. The Robinsons' workmen began to plant windbreaks, and to furrow flat land to make it unusable by airplanes.

On Pearl Harbor Day—Sunday, December 7, 1941—a Japanese fighter plane, disabled over Oahu, came down on Niihau. For the island, which was quite without speedy means of communication, this was the first intimation that there was a war on. The pilot, though shaken up, survived the emergency landing; before he recovered, however, the Niihauans took him prisoner and got hold of his papers. The Robinsons' supply boat was expected shortly from Kauai, but the Kauai military authorities ordered them not to make the trip that week, and so the pilot had to be held on Niihau for several days. On December 12 he escaped from his makeshift prison with the help of a Japanese resident of Niihau named Harada, who worked for the Robinsons as a beekeeper and handyman. The pilot recovered his pistol, and Harada carried a shotgun, the only other weapon on Niihau. Aware of the danger, the Niihau men got their families out of harm's way while the two Japanese searched the deserted village for the pilot's papers, taken at the time of his crash. Frustrated, they burned one of the village houses. About dawn of the next day a Hawaiian named Benehakaka Kanahele, along with his wife, decided to see what was going on. They had just reached the village when they were captured by Harada and the pilot, still in possession of the island's only firearms.

The Kanaheles were kept under surveillance by the Japanese for some time. Then Benehakaka, a very large man, seized a split-second opportunity and attacked the pilot. His wife grappled with Harada. The pilot pulled his pistol out of his boot and shot Kanahele three times before the huge Hawaiian picked him up and threw him with tremendous force against a stone wall, killing him. Kanahele then turned on Harada, who instantly shot himself in the stomach with the shotgun. The fighting war on Niihau was over. Kanahele, with three bullets in him, walked back to the village, to survive as Niihau's only winner of the Purple Heart.

After the war the territorial legislature declared itself determined that Niihau should not continue in its old condition. A Senate committee went on an investigative tour, and brought in an adverse report announcing that the entire community of Niihau was out of step with the times. Long before, in the 1890's,

CULVER PICTURES

Honolulu looked like this when the Sinclair family, soon to become Niihau's owners, arrived in the Islands in 1863.

Francis Gay, one of the clan, had made a public statement of the family's attitude toward the Hawaiians of his day. He characterized them as ease-loving, cheerful, generous, and amiable, but irresponsible, lacking in forethought, pliant, and terribly susceptible to political corruption. "It is perfectly impossible," he said, "that they should be able to form any estimate of the needs of an intelligent and civilised country; many of them, enfranchised citizens, . . . still live on fish and poi." There was nothing unusual in this point of view at the time; and given its assumptions, there was a clear need for stewardship of the kind exercised by his family.

In the 1940's the Robinsons remained paternalistic in their attitude toward the Hawaiians, but in the meantime many things had changed around them. The Senate committee, whose chairman had Hawaiian blood, found the stewardship still in effect—baneful effect. Niihauans, they said, lived in complete subservience to the owners of the island; and "kindly and paternal as the dominion of their landlords is, it is still irreconcilable with the principles of liberty and the freedom of individuals upon which our Nation was founded . . ." In the committee's opinion, no one born and raised on Niihau would have a chance of decent survival in competition with free men in the Hawaiian Islands or the Union generally.

Here was a new declaration of war; and a long-drawn-out battle of attrition began in which the territorial legislature made marginal gains without ever completing what it saw as its duty—to bring Niihau into line with the rest of the Islands. There was strong support for the Robinsons among leaders of the Hawaiian community.

After 1945 the island tenants continued to work for the Robinsons, living in their archaic style, earning between one and three thousand dollars a year, owning little property other than their horses, living in Robinson-supplied wooden houses, eating Robinson-supplied food. Everyone had house and garden free of charge, whether there was a breadwinner in the family or not. They saw less of the Robinson clan than their grandfathers had. Aylmer Robinson, bachelor son of a marriage between Aubrey Robinson and a cousin, Alice Gay, made regular trips to the island, but no one lived permanently in the old homestead, and it stood quietly deteriorating, its garden undisciplined and its turn-of-the-century library yellowing on the bookshelves.

Hawaiian foremen supervised the daily work; and the Robinson social policy was administered by the preachers and elders of the native church and the schoolteachers, chosen by the Robinsons from among island residents. Standard English-language texts were used in Niihau's school, but the language of work, worship, and play was, as always, Hawaiian; the alien tongue continued to be discarded after children left school. As a result of increased attention from the territory, the school extended its services to the eighth grade, but even so no Niihauan ever managed to pass a modern armed services literacy test.

The muscular strength of the Niihauans was itself deceptive. Hawaiians as a race continued to be highly susceptible to heart and vascular disease, and Niihauans as much as Hawaiians elsewhere. Niihau's diet in the postwar years was overstocked with canned goods and bottled soda, along with the traditional fish and poi, turkeys and hogs hunted on the island, rice in enormous quantities brought from Kauai, and vegetables grown in plots at Puuwai village. Niihauans overate—eight thousand pounds of poi alone in an average month for two hundred and fifty people; and this added to their health problems.

The forties, fifties, and sixties brought with them a certain level of material modernity. Some families bought gas-operated refrigerators. The Robinsons finally installed a radio-telephone linking Niihau with Makaweli, supplementing but not superseding the carrier pigeons and signal-fire beacons used for decades. Niihauans spent some of their money on mail-order goods, and many cowboys went out on the job carrying transistor radios tuned to Kauai and Honolulu stations. A few years ago a California scientist collecting shallow-water fish off Niihau was sociably waved ashore for a conversation by two Hawaiian cowboys. One had his radio with him. It was broadcasting the Dow-Jones industrial index, but the information must have been esoteric, since the Hawaiian had no clear idea where the American mainland was.

One area in which Robinson control remained totally unimpaired was politics. Ever since the first elections under the territory at the turn of the century, the Niihauans had voted solidly Republican. Up through the twenties there were a few stray votes for Home Rulers and Democrats, but in the thirties these virtually disappeared. When the statehood plebiscite was held in June, 1959, Niihau was the only precinct in the whole of the Hawaiian Islands to vote against full membership in the Union. Residents of Hawaii took part in a presidential election for the first time in 1960, and patriotic pride in the occasion was high. The turnout was impressive, the accuracy of the tallying less so. Successively announced "official final" figures veered almost with the trade winds. Kennedy ultimately won Hawaii's three electoral college votes on a recount; but for a day or two it looked almost as if Niihau's 99-to-0 vote for Nixon would carry the Islands for the Republicans.

This kind of monolithic behavior at the polls had previously prompted state Democrats to question Niihau's election procedures. They were particularly interested to learn that no authorized election inspector from the Democratic party was ever present when votes were counted. Again, on the figures, no Niihauan ever spoiled a ballot—the same people who failed the armed forces literacy test passed the effective test of political literacy. All through the period of American rule, ballots in the Islands had been printed in Hawaiian and English, so that the Niihauans' inability to cope with the major language of American politics would not necessarily disqualify them from voting validly. But on nearby Kauai, an island with a much more effective educational system, spoiled ballots ran about ten per cent in an average election. Questioned on the matter a few years ago, Aylmer Robinson said he was a Republican, though by no means a solid party man, and Niihauans also happened to be Republicans. His family took no interest in politics, he said; they merely arranged for election supplies to be taken to the island, and for the results to be flown out again by carrier pigeon—nothing more. He was sure that the election inspectors were men of integrity. He might have added that no political rallies, or even election posters, have ever been seen on Niihau.

As in prewar years, access to the island remained limited; the only regular connection was by Robinson sampan from Kauai, and the family dictated absolutely the composition of each load of passengers. Relatives and friends of the Niihauans could make visits of up to a few weeks, but even in this case the Robinsons discouraged extended stays. Politicians and civil servants with legitimate credentials were allowed to carry out their assignments; and scholars and scientists were assisted by the Robinsons. Publicity was shunned as always; and the press was totally excluded except on very rare occasions, such as a governor's tour.

This restriction was occasionally subverted. In 1957 a newspaperman flying over Niihau in a light plane was forced to crash-land; providentially, he was carrying his camera. Again, in 1960, a bearded reporter paid some Kauai fishermen to take him to Niihau and put him ashore before daybreak. His presence (but not his profession) was reported to Aylmer Robinson, who made a special trip to remove the "vagrant" to Kauai. The Robinsons, justifiably enough, complained to the reporter's newspaper about the trouble caused by the incident.

All this gave something of a sharp edge to attempts, originating in the Democratic party, to bring Niihau to conformity with the rest of the territory. Not long after World War II, researchers discovered a legal circumstance which, on the face of things, gave the territory title to some lands on Niihau. The position was this: statute law at the time of the sale to the Sinclairs provided that school and church sites could not be disposed of to private buyers as long as they were being used for their intended purpose. There were certainly school sites on Niihau in the 1860's, according to teachers' running reports—four in 1862, three in 1865, two in 1866, and one (at Puuwai village) in 1867. But the whole issue remained clouded because for the crucial years of 1863 and 1864, the years of the Sinclair takeover, no documents could be found in public repositories.

All through the second half of the nineteenth century and into the twentieth, the clan and the government co-operated to maintain roads on Niihau. Government money was spent on this and on installations at a landing pier; and these facts too were made the basis for government claims against the Robinsons.

Action proceeded slowly, hampered by lack of continuity of personnel in the attorney general's office and in legislative committees. The Robinson family, of course, showed no interest in initiating activity. Reports were filed, surveys projected, further investigations ordered; but the position remained substantially what it was when the Senate committee brought back its disparaging report just after World War II.

Massive inertia in regard to changing control of land has been characteristic of Hawaiian politics ever since the growth of the great estates late in the nineteenth century; and the Niihau case, in one of its aspects, is merely a reflection of this.

In the meantime the Niihauans live on, happy in their day-to-day life, and, as always, affectionately respectful to Aylmer Robinson. In 1963 he is a spare and vigorous seventy-five-year-old, unshaken in his conviction of righteousness in his dealings with his charges. Change is inevitable, but it will occur at an evolutionary rate as long as Aylmer Robinson stands between Niihau and the outside. The Niihauans themselves recognize that they are different, not only from the rest of the world but also from other Hawaiians. In their non-English-speaking microcosm, they have kept the speech patterns that were peculiar to their end of the island chain in pre-white days, though the allegorical richness of classical Hawaiian thought and expression has long since withered away. In their church they celebrate God in Hawaiian-language hymns of their own composition; their secular festivals are not the holidays observed by most Americans, but birthdays and other occasions of a simple, basic sort. In numerous other ways their universe is bounded by their coast line.

It seems, oddly enough, that change may be forced

Modern in most of their customs, Hawaiians on the larger islands still surfboard much as they did a century ago.

upon Niihau by conditions over which even the Robinsons cannot exercise control. Over the last decade the economy of the island has been faltering. There were several years of drought between 1950 and 1960, and as water sources dried up, the cattle and sheep population had to be cut back sharply. A cactus blight, introduced on Kauai, where the plant had become a pest, spread to Niihau, where cactus had been one of the principal stock feeds on arid grazing land. This further cut down herds and also lessened the number of wild pigs. A parasite attacked the blossoms of the keawe tree, essential to the honey industry, and production fell off badly. Commercial fishing off the island greatly reduced the Niihauans' own catches. In drought years Niihau wool, one of the big exports, was at a disadvantage in a competitive market: it was burr-laden and stained by dry red dust; and because of lack of water it could not be washed before export. Hard to sell, it sometimes stayed in storage for seasons before being moved.

Faced with multiple problems, Aylmer Robinson tried to revive the economy. Egyptian cotton would grow very well on Niihau, but the federal government refused the island a quota. Keawe wood made excellent charcoal, but Japan could undersell Niihau on the west coast of the United States. Old Hawaiian fish-breeding ponds were restored to offset losses caused by commercial fishermen, but the principal product was mosquitoes. The situation is made more critical by the fact that Niihau, alone among rural areas in Hawaii, has been in the middle of a minor population explosion, and though the Robinsons have kept every man on the payroll there is clearly no economic justification for maintaining the island in its present condition.

Should the economy cease to be viable, the Niihauans would find it very difficult to take up life anywhere in Hawaii except at the Robinson ranch on Kauai. Over the course of the years, some Niihauans have moved away and found work on other plantations, on the Honolulu waterfront, and on inter-island ships. But in the event of a final exodus, a long-range educational program, in English, would be necessary to fit everybody—men, women, and children—for normal existence on the outside. This, of course, could not begin to take account of all the adjustments they would have to make, and its very inauguration would depend on the word of Aylmer Robinson, whose whole life has been dedicated to slowing the rate of change on Niihau. His grand plan has always been, as he explained to an Interior Department official in 1946, to preserve intact the Hawaiian cultural pattern. In practice this meant preserving not pre-white Hawaiian culture, but the missionary culture of the nineteenth century, transmitted in the native language, and leaving language alone reasonably intact among the native institutions. Even with this limitation, however, the Robinsons' efforts in behalf of the diminished Hawaiian race have far outstripped those of the state government.

The Niihauans have no real sense of the past that was theirs before 1864, when the Sinclairs bought their land; and they have at most an uncertain future. They concentrate their best hopes upon their Protestant God, and at the same time they continue to show an unswerving trust in the Robinsons, believing that no harm can befall them as long as the *haku* watches over them from Makaweli, where a great window in the west wall of the old home frames a hundred years of island history, poignantly quiet across the water.

Gavan Daws is at work on a history of Honolulu which will be his doctoral dissertation at the University of Hawaii. Timothy Head is a research fellow with the East-West Center of the same institution.

The American Eagle

HARDWARE

The art of window dressing, in our opinion, is in a dreadful state of decline today. Simple, elegant, austere: this is the new *ton*. We were reminded of this fact recently when we chanced upon a little brown book which recalls the art in its heyday. It has a catchy title: *The American Hardware Store: A Manual of Approved Methods of Arranging and Displaying Hardware,* and it was written by one R. R. Williams in 1892.

Williams was no wild-eyed visionary. As he said quite pointedly in his book, "The primary object of windows is to give the necessary light to the interior of the store." With that fact established, he moved on to a new proposition: Why leave anything on a shelf when it can work for you out front?

Household Wants, '92 Model

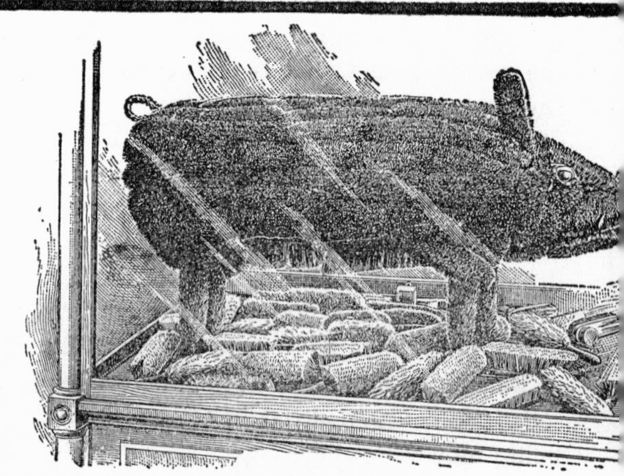

A Brush Exhibit

Horse and Sleigh—A Unique Window Display

FANTASIA

His pictures show how. That cutlery eagle is all spoons save for the French cooking knives in his tail and wings, which are seven feet wide from tip to tip. The extravaganza at lower right uses planes for the face, hands, and feet, plainly permitting the pun in the sign, "Plain Planing by a Plain Man." The pig made from brushes? The "Saw Bicycle"? Easy enough. It was with "Household Wants" and "Horse and Sleigh," where pudding pans and oil heaters double as faces and bodies, that Williams rose to his full artistic height. Surely modern window dressers could profit from studying the techniques of this old master and approaching windows with his plucky attitude. "Give me the tools," he seems to say to the world, "and I will finish the job."

The American Eagle—Rear View

A Saw Bicycle

A Show Window Carpenter Shop

The Tragic Dream of Jean Ribaut CONTINUED FROM PAGE 15

vindicated Philip II's decision to de-emphasize the mainland, and Spain made no further serious efforts to gain a permanent foothold there.

But in France, meanwhile, the Truce of Amboise granted the Huguenots a temporary breathing spell. Unable to forget the allure of the New World with its promise of a Protestant haven, Huguenot leaders began making plans to send out another expedition. Since Ribaut was still imprisoned in England, the leadership of the second voyage to America passed to Laudonnière, the observant and articulate chronicler of the first trip. On April 22, 1564, he departed from Le Havre with a fleet of three ships. Like Ribaut's first voyage, Laudonnière's was essentially military in character. Of the 300 people accompanying him, 110 were sailors, 120 were soldiers, and the rest were artisans, servants, and page boys. There were also four women aboard and, as might have been expected, this caused trouble.

Laudonnière raised the coast of Florida on June 22, then proceeded to the River of May, where the Indians greeted him like a returning prodigal. To Laudonnière's amazement, they had carefully tended the stone pillar erected by Ribaut two years earlier; more, they had been worshipping it. "Wee found the same crowned with crownes of Bay, and at the foote thereof many little baskets full of Mill which they call in their language Tapaga Tapola," Laudonnière wrote. "Then when they came thither they kissed the same with great reverence and besought us to do the like, which we would not denie them, to the ende we might drawe them to be more in friendship with us."

Laudonnière explored the coast to the north, but turned back before reaching the abandoned site at Port Royal. He decided to make his permanent headquarters with the friendly savages at the mouth of the May River. Here he built a sizable compound which he named Fort Caroline.

Despite the happy homecoming, Laudonnière's problems at Fort Caroline soon began to accumulate almost faster than he could handle them. Within three months of his arrival he was stricken with a fever, probably malaria, that sapped him of his strength throughout his stay in Florida. Several mutinies broke out. One group of dissident settlers tried to poison Laudonnière; when this plot failed they attempted to blow him up by placing a keg of gunpowder under his sickbed. A short time later, two shallops that the sailors had recently built were stolen by mutineers, who then embarked on a career of piracy.

Laudonnière aggravated his situation by making the same basic error that the garrison at Charlesfort had made: he relied too heavily on the generosity of the Indians. When winter came, the modest granaries of the neighboring tribes were exhausted; the Frenchmen had to forage for roots and bargain with distant peoples to stave off starvation. Inevitably, the Indians rebelled against these constant demands. Under the leadership of a powerful chief named Outina, they finally attacked a French foraging party, killing two and wounding twenty-two others.

With some justification, Laudonnière attributed his difficulties to the lack of support from home. "For if wee had bene succoured in time & place, & according to the promise that was made unto us, the warre which was between us and Outina, had not fallen out," he complained. "Neither should wee have had occasion to offend the Indians, which with all paines in the world I entertained in good amitie."

Reports of the unrest at Fort Caroline had meanwhile reached the homeland via a French ship that had called there in the fall of 1564. Distance seems to have magnified the bill of particulars against the unfortunate Laudonnière; he was reported to be living in sin with one of the four women on the expedition and was said to be acting like a tyrant, even trying to set himself up as king.

Jean Ribaut, now out of prison and back in France itching to return to America, was commissioned to lead a third expedition to Florida and take over command from Laudonnière. He left Le Havre on May 10, 1565, with five vessels carrying some 600 soldiers, laborers, women, and children. Unlike the two previous expeditions, this was a full-fledged colonizing effort. Commanding one of the ships in Jean Ribaut's train was his son Jacques, like his father a captain in the French Navy.

Unknown to the French, there was trouble ahead. Two months after Ribaut left Le Havre, a Spanish force departed from Cadiz under the command of Pedro Menéndez de Avilés, one of the ablest admirals in the Spanish fleet. His destination was also Florida, and his orders directed him to find out "whether there are on said coast or country, any settlers who are corsairs, or of any other nations not subject to us." If this proved to be true (and Menéndez knew it was, for the intelligence pipeline between Spain and France was working better), he was bluntly ordered to "cast them out by the best means that seems to you possible." Though the two countries were still at peace, a battle fought in far-off Florida could be diplomatically swept under the rug if it proved to be embarrassing in Europe.

After dawdling for a considerable length of time to explore more rivers, Ribaut arrived at Fort Caroline on August 28. Here at last was the succor the ailing Laudonnière had been longing for. But events set in motion three years before by the first French inroads into what Spain considered her exclusive territory were now rapidly moving to a climax. A week after Ribaut's arrival, six Spanish warships appeared off the coast near the mouth of the May River.

Though Ribaut was on shore, the men aboard his ships cut their anchor chains and put to sea. The Spaniards gave chase, but were rapidly outdistanced by the smaller, faster French vessels. As the Spanish ships headed back toward the coast, the French fleet shadowed them, found they had put into St. Augustine's harbor, some thirty-five miles to the south, and then reported back to Ribaut.

Always the man of action, Ribaut ordered all able-bodied men at Fort Caroline aboard his ships to pursue the enemy. Laudonnière protested that this would leave him defenseless against an overland attack, but Ribaut was now in command. On September 10, leaving two ships behind, he set sail to attack Menéndez, who meanwhile had disembarked his forces at St. Augustine and begun to fortify his position.

Among the many things discovered in the New World—tobacco, corn, pumpkins, turkeys—most history books fail to make note of the hurricane. Peculiar to the east coast of North America (and to the east coast of Asia, most of which was *terra incognita* in 1565), the hurricane posed problems that the European seaman was totally unable to cope with. Its portents—high cirrus "mare's-tails" in the sky, the ominous calm, the first fitful, nervous gusts—had not as yet been related to the ferocity that was likely to follow. Once caught in a hurricane with its contradictory winds and mountainous waves, the most experienced and able European sailors were in a realm that had existed heretofore only in the imaginations of madmen. Shortly after Ribaut made his first contact with the Spanish at St. Augustine, a hurricane struck.

The great tempest wrecked three of his ships. With great difficulty, he and 600 of his men made it to shore near the harbor, where the Spanish fleet had safely ridden out the storm. Though Menéndez did not yet know of the extent of the catastrophe that had befallen Ribaut, he surmised that the French fleet had been badly scattered.

After a swift overland march, Menéndez attacked Fort Caroline early on the morning of September 20. Routed out in their nightshirts, Laudonnière's small garrison were unable to put up any effective resistance and fled through the marshes in an attempt to reach the two ships that, anchored in the river, had survived the hurricane. By nightfall the Spanish had killed 132 Frenchmen without suffering a single casualty. The survivors were few: Laudonnière, the artist Le Moyne, the woman who had caused Laudonnière so much grief, and eighteen or twenty others. They were taken aboard the two ships, one of which was commanded by Ribaut's son, and hastily set sail for France.

Meanwhile Jean Ribaut and his men, stranded on the hot Florida beaches without food, water, or arms, began to surrender a few at a time. They were asked, "Are you Catholics or Lutherans, and are there any who wish to confess?" All but a few remained stout Huguenots to the bitter end and they were led out behind the dunes and summarily executed. On October 10 Ribaut himself and the last remnants of his force capitulated. They too were put to death. For an epitaph on his unknown grave, the remarkable Ribaut might have had the words of his executioner, Pedro Menéndez: "The King of France could do more with him with fifty thousand ducats, than with others with five hundred thousand; and he could do more in one year than another in ten, for he was the most experienced seaman and corsair known."

And so ended France's ill-starred attempts to colonize the east coast of what would become the United States. Now the die was cast: the departure of the French from Fort Caroline marked the beginning of the pattern that was to shape North America for all time.

Under Pedro Menéndez, the Spanish settlement at St. Augustine took hold; Spain was to dominate Florida until she ceded it to the United States in 1821. As a precaution, the Spanish twice attempted to establish outposts at the site of Ribaut's first settlement at Port Royal, but as their influence began to wane and the

CULVER PICTURES

The massacre of Ribaut, in a nineteenth-century engraving

English began to push farther south from Virginia, these forts were abandoned, leaving as their only legacy "tabby," a kind of concrete the Spaniards had learned to make from oyster shells; copied by the English, it may still be seen in the foundations of the older homes of the lower South Carolina coast.

The French, following the lead of Jacques Cartier, now shifted their attention to Canada and began pushing down the Mississippi Valley and up from New Orleans. Today the only testaments to their dramatic moves to colonize South Carolina and Florida are two monuments, one at the site of Fort Caroline on the St. Johns River near present-day Jacksonville, the other on the seaward tip of Parris Island, South Carolina, home of the famous U.S. Marine Corps "boot camp," where Charlesfort is believed to have stood. (The exact location of Charlesfort is still much disputed. Evidence recently unearthed suggests that it may have been on nearby Port Royal Island—*Ed.*)

A few place names—monuments of a less formal nature—tell a different story. Ribaut's "fayrest and greatest haven" in South Carolina is still known as Port Royal. And down on the east coast of Florida, an inlet near St. Augustine is still called Matanzas. In Spanish the word means slaughter, and near here lie the bones of Jean Ribaut, a man who might have altered the course of American history were it not for a hurricane.

Port Royal and its environs are home country to Sherwood Harris, who was raised in nearby Beaufort, South Carolina. Mr. Harris, formerly a member of the Saturday Evening Post's *Washington bureau, resigned in 1960 to devote his time to free-lance writing.*

For further reading: Jean Ribaut, Together with a Transcript of an English Version in the British Museum, *by Jeannette Thurber Connor (Florida State Historical Society, 1927);* The Land Called Chicora, *by Paul Quattlebaum (University of Florida Press, 1956).*

The Strike That Made a President

CONTINUED FROM PAGE 47

eligible for a sinecure: a directorship in some life insurance company or the peace of the First National Bank.

Storrow and the members of the Citizens' Committee spent a baffling weekend trying to locate the Governor. They themselves wanted no open break with the police. Their compromise plan, approved by Mayor Peters, would have allowed an unaffiliated union. If the men would call off their strike there would be no disciplinary action taken against the leaders, and the various other grievances would be submitted to an impartial board. The counsel for the union urged the membership to accept. If the Governor and the Commissioner had agreed, they would undoubtedly have done so. But Curtis declined to accept any solution "that might be construed as a pardon of the men on trial." On Monday morning he suspended the nineteen police leaders.

Peters, as fluttery and ineffectual as ever, scurried about trying to find some last-minute solution, although by now he was convinced that the strike was unavoidable. As mayor he had the right in an emergency to call out the units of the State Guard within the Boston area. Characteristically, he was not aware of this.

Coolidge returned suddenly to his office on Monday afternoon in a testy mood; at about the same time the police were voting, 1,134 to 2, to strike on the following day at five o'clock. Monday evening Coolidge had dinner with Storrow, Peters, and several members of the Citizens' Committee in a private room of the Union Club. Before the dinner Storrow and Peters begged the Governor to sponsor the compromise plan as the last hope of averting the strike. He refused. Finally they asked him to mobilize three or four thousand troops of the State Guard. He maintained that the situation could be left safely in Curtis' hands. In spite of the overwhelming vote to strike, Curtis still felt that the majority of the police would remain loyal to him.

Meanwhile, after a series of calls from Peters, the adjutant general, Jesse Stevens, decided that a certain amount of preparation might be wise after all and sent out verbal orders for the State Guard's only mounted squadron to assemble at the Commonwealth Armory. Coolidge learned of this minor mobilization several hours after the Union Club dinner. Knowing by politician's instinct that to call out the militia prematurely is political suicide, he telephoned Curtis and angrily started for the Armory.

With a pale and silent Curtis just behind him, Coolidge strode through the Armory arch. A hundred or so troopers were standing about on the lower floor and stared in surprise at their irate Governor, who quacked at the commanding officer, Major Dana Gallup, "Who told you people to come here? Go home!" With that he stalked petulantly up the stairs to the orderly room, followed by Gallup and Curtis.

Public fears about the police strike were summed up in a cartoon by Rollin Kirby of the New York World.

Then occurred one of the most dramatic, if hitherto unrecorded, minor episodes of the strike. Peters, repulsed and desperate, had set out in frantic pursuit of Coolidge. Ten minutes after the Governor arrived, the rumpled and excited Mayor burst through the Armory door demanding to see him. At that very moment Coolidge was coming down the stairs. The two men faced each other, Peters stammering accusations until Coolidge cut him short with a waspish, "You have no business here."

At that Peters made a rush for him, swinging his arms wildly and somehow landing a punch square on the Governor's left eye. Coolidge did not attempt to strike back, nor did he make any move to retreat, but merely stood there with his hand to his face. Troopers at once seized the gesticulating Mayor. It was fortunate for the Governor that he was not called on to make many public appearances that week, for those who saw him could not fail to notice his obvious shiner.

Peters, Curtis, and Coolidge were all at their desks on Tuesday morning. At one o'clock in the afternoon the Mayor called the Commissioner, who assured him he had ample means to protect the city. Four hours later—just as the policemen were ready to walk out—the three key figures held a last acid conference. To Peters' renewed plea to call out the State Guard, Coolidge ironically replied that the mayor had the power to summon local units. But Curtis still insisted he did not need the State Guard.

Of the 1,544 men in the Boston police department, 1,117 went out on strike. There was no authority on hand to replace them. Although a force of citizen volunteers had been enrolling in the preceding weeks, the Commissioner did not use them. Years later, Coolidge wrote in his autobiography that he felt afterward he should have called out the State Guard as soon as the police left their posts. "The Commissioner," he added as an apologia, "did not feel that this was necessary." Peters, faced with a sudden decision, could not bring himself to muster local guard units. The strike was left to follow its own pattern unimpeded.

As the police left the station houses, still in uniform but minus their badges, they were cheered by some, and a few furtive adolescents crept up to throw mud against the station doors. At first nothing more happened. Then in the twilight little groups began to start dice games all over Boston Common. From the top of Beacon Hill they looked like mushrooms springing up on the slope by the Frog Pond as they formed circles to shoot craps under the shadow of the Statehouse. It was harmless enough at first, a naïve gesture against authority. But with the darkness crowds began to gather on the other side of Beacon Hill in the vicinity of Scollay Square with its honky-tonks and flophouses. For some time they milled about restlessly, as yet uncertain, waiting only for that unifying act of violence that would turn them into a mob. Then it happened. As with all such events no one could be quite sure afterward how it started—a store window was broken, a truck overturned, a woman screamed, and the mob was off.

The Boston mob that first night was truculent but aimless. Around Scollay Square plate-glass windows were smashed and stores looted. Pedestrians had their hats knocked off, there were scattered hold-ups in open view, and later in the evening several women were dragged into doorways and assaulted. Some of the streetcar lines were blocked with mattresses and railroad ties. In the Celtic matrix of South Boston the unfocussed rowdyism confined itself to such japes as stoning the empty police stations and pulling the trolleys off the wires. But there was a sinister air about the carnival in those milling streets.

Tuesday night Peters vanished as effectively as Coolidge had over the weekend. Then late Wednesday morning he finally called out the State Guard in Boston, and before the end of the afternoon the guardsmen were patrolling the streets. Peters soon after issued a statement to the press remarking plaintively that in this crisis he had "received no co-operation from the Police Commissioner and no help or practical suggestions from the Governor." Now, with the authority he claimed to have found under an old statute, he removed Curtis and began calling up citizen volunteers.

To those businessmen who received badge and revolver from the downtown police stations the strike was an adventure. For once again, if briefly, the old Bostonians had achieved physical control of their city. As one leafs through the old newspaper files one sees them in faded rotogravure, smiling, self-assured faces, the younger men dressed in trench coats copied from those of wartime British officers. Here and there one finds a sterner note: some Beacon Hill relic of the Civil War days patrolling the financial district with golf cap and night stick. Ex-Harvard athletes-turned-broker are abundant.

During the day the city remained quiet, but Wednesday evening the mob gathered again, a harder and more menacing mob than the night before. Many of its members were armed, and the ranks were reinforced by professional criminals who had been heading toward Boston all the afternoon. Striking policemen moved through the crowd, encouraging the more violent. Behind the closed doors of the banks and the larger stores, blocked off now by barbed wire, employees stood ready with pistols and rifles. In Scollay Square, at the center of the disorders, steel-helmeted guardsmen advancing across the cobbles with fixed bayonets were showered with bricks, stones, and bottles. Not far from the site of the Boston Massacre, they finally opened fire on their assailants, killing three. Near Cornhill four Harvard undergraduates, acting as volunteer policemen, were almost lynched. On the other side of Beacon Hill several guard companies cleared the unruly Common in a flanking movement, rounding up the surly groups still gathered there. Somehow a sailor was killed in the scuffle. Two other men were killed in South Boston. After that the mob melted away.

The Citizens' Committee reported that "by Thursday morning order had generally been restored in the city." The strike was broken. Coolidge had been consulting with Murray Crane and the Republican elders, all of whom felt it was now time to take a stand. So, nettled by the Mayor's statement and by the removal of the Police Commissioner, Coolidge belatedly acted. By executive order he called out the entire State Guard and assumed full control over the Boston police department, instructing Curtis to resume his post at once.

BOSTON *Herald*, NOVEMBER 4, 1919

On the day of the Massachusetts gubernatorial election of 1919 this cartoon, captioned "The Pilot Who Weathered the Storm" appeared in the Boston Herald, *commenting on Calvin Coolidge's role in the police strike two months earlier. Apparently it reflected the opinion of a majority of the commonwealth's voters: the "pilot" was re-elected in a landslide, defeating his Democratic opponent 317,794 to 192,673.*

After the rioting the strike had overshadowed all other news, capturing the headlines and alarming newspaper readers throughout the country. By the time it had made its full impact Coolidge had taken over. At once this Yankee governor with the dour expression became a national figure. His pictures papered the land. Even President Wilson sent him a letter of congratulation. And when the Governor replied to President Samuel Gompers of the A. F. of L., who had asked reinstatement of the strikers, he proclaimed: "There is no right to strike against the public safety by anybody, anywhere, any time." Whatever Peters and the members of the committee might think, Coolidge became, in the words of the Boston *Herald,* "the pilot who weathered the storm."

On Friday the striking policemen, dismayed by the reaction against them, voted almost unanimously to return to work on the same basis as before the strike. They had counted on organized labor to back them up, but the two days' rioting had made public opinion too hostile. Commissioner Curtis would have nothing to do with them. He issued an order that none of the striking policemen would ever be taken back—and none ever were. Instead he raised the minimum wage to $1,400 a year and began recruiting a new force.

Meanwhile the volunteers were sent home, and all Boston police duties were carried on by the State Guard. At the time, the Guard was still largely the temporary organization of overage and underage men who had joined when the regular Massachusetts National Guard—the Yankee Division—had been called to active service in 1917. The guardsmen's aspect was ludicrously unmilitary. They scarcely knew the manual of arms, and they still wore the laced leggings and felt campaign hats of the Mexican Border Campaign of 1916 that had been replaced in the A.E.F. by spiral puttees and overseas caps.

By the end of the year Commissioner Curtis had recruited his new police force, and the olive-drab uniforms of the State Guard disappeared from the city's streets. Before the strike the police of Boston still wore dome-shaped gray helmets like those of the English bobbies and high-necked frock coats above which protruded the ends of a wing collar. With their leather outer belts and long wooden night sticks they resembled the old Keystone Cops. The new police had different uniforms. The long coats and wing collars were discarded. Caps replaced the helmets. It was the close of an era, the end of the patrolman walking his beat under the gas lamps past the corner saloon, the beginning of prowl cars and bootleg gin.

For Calvin Coolidge it was a new beginning, too. In the 1918 election he had defeated the Democratic candidate, Richard H. Long, by less than 17,000 votes. Two months after the police strike the Governor overwhelmed Long, who had attacked his handling of it, by more than 125,000, the final tally being 317,794 to 192,673. There were whisperings of Coolidge as a dark-horse presidential candidate in 1920. "Jack the Giant Killer," William Allen White called him.

To entrenched party elders like Henry Cabot Lodge, who were under no illusions about the actual role Coolidge had played in the police strike, the notion of their escalator governor as the Republican candidate for President was an absurdity. "Nominate a man who lives in a two-family house!" Senator Lodge exploded with Brahmin hauteur. "Never! Massachusetts is not for him!"

There was one man in Boston, however, who long before the strike had envisioned Coolidge in the White House, and to enliven that vision he was willing to devote his time, his energies, and his considerable fortune. Frank W. Stearns, the friendly, fussy little merchant who had inherited the very proper Bostonian department store of R. H. Stearns, first met Coolidge when the latter was merely president of the Massachusetts Senate. Stearns had at once been struck by qualities apparent to few others. Over the years he made himself laughable by announcing to all hearers that Coolidge was a second Abraham Lincoln who would end up as President of the United States. The editor of the *Herald* finally accused Stearns of trying to create a character out of Coolidge the way Dickens had of Martin Chuzzlewit. Stearns was impervious to witticisms. To him Calvin Coolidge was the greatest man in public life in Massachusetts, perhaps in America.

Some months before the police strike Stearns had completed financial arrangements with Houghton Mifflin to publish a book of twenty or so speeches made by Coolidge as lieutenant governor, to be called *Bay State Orations*. They were at best pithy platitudes, for if Coolidge had no great originality of mind, his style was at least brief and to the point. A Houghton Mifflin editor cleverly conceived of taking a phrase from a speech to give the book the arresting title of *Have Faith in Massachusetts*. It appeared, like a reinforcement, shortly after the police strike. Several thousand copies were sold, and Stearns gave away over 65,000 more. With the June Republican National Convention in mind, he saw to it that an autographed copy went to every G.O.P. delegate and alternate in the country.

If the Republican presidential nomination of 1920 had been awarded by popular vote it would have gone to General Leonard Wood, by far the outstanding candidate. But it was obvious before the Chicago convention that Wood, although he controlled the largest single bloc of delegates, would obtain no early majority. His chief opponent was Frank Lowden, another able man, with a distinguished record in Congress and as Governor of Illinois. The politicians-behind-the-scenes were convinced that neither Wood nor Lowden could win, that in the end they would cancel each other out.

Cautious Coolidge stayed away from Chicago and refused to announce his candidacy, even though most of the Massachusetts delegates were pledged to him. Just before the convention, Stearns opened and presided over a modest headquarters at Chicago's Congress Hotel. He presented each arriving delegate with a small pamphlet of sixty pages containing excerpts from Coolidge's speeches. Bound in imitation black leather, it was entitled *Law and Order.*

The convention opened in the barnlike, reverberating Chicago Coliseum on Tuesday, June 8. Four hundred and ninety-three votes were necessary to win the nomination, out of a total of 984. On the first ballot, taken on Friday, June 11, Wood received 287½ votes, Lowden 211½, and Coolidge, in seventh place, 34. By the fourth ballot Wood had reached 314 votes, with Lowden fixed at 289. The expected deadlock had arrived. To the surprise and anger of the delegates, and amid a rising chorus of boos, Chairman Henry Cabot Lodge adjourned the convention. That night, in the legendary "smoke-filled room" at the Blackstone Hotel, the party bosses tapped the shoulder of Senator Warren G. Harding of Ohio, and late the following afternoon, on the tenth ballot, he was nominated.

There was, of course, still the minor matter of the vice presidential candidate to consider. During the roll call for the tenth ballot, the senatorial hierarchs huddled in a small alcove concealed under the speakers' stand and decided on Irvine Lenroot of Wisconsin. Besides being a trusted senator, Lenroot would add a mildly liberal balance to Harding's machine conservatism. It was arranged that Senator Medill McCormick of Illinois would make the nominating speech, to be seconded by H. L. Remmel, an old-line politician from Arkansas. The word was passed along to the delegates, some of whom were already drifting out of the darkening hall.

Senator McCormick duly mounted the platform and in a perfunctory two-minute speech nominated Lenroot. The florid old pro Remmel seconded the nomination. With contemptuous indifference Senator Lodge turned over the gavel to ex-Governor Frank Willis of Ohio, and he and McCormick left the platform. The vast Coliseum echoed with the loud tramp and shuffle of feet, the clatter of chairs as more and more of the delegates and onlookers in the galleries made their way toward the exits.

Scarcely anyone could catch what the speakers were saying, nor did it seem to matter. Suddenly on the far side of the hall a stocky, red-faced man climbed on a chair and bellowed for recognition. Affably, the substitute chairman recognized Wallace McCamant of Oregon, assuming that his was merely one more seconding voice for Lenroot.

There is a moment when the whip cracks and the animal, instead of jumping, turns on the ringmaster. Chairman Willis did not recognize that moment until it was too late. The voice from the floor was no casual approval of an accomplished fact. McCamant had talked the matter over angrily with his delegation and decided to have none of Lenroot. In the last year he had been sent three complimentary copies of *Have Faith in Massachusetts.* Coolidge was the man he thought of now, "Law and Order" Coolidge.

McCamant's voice rumbled on in undistinguishable phrases, then broke clear with: "I name for the exalted office of Vice President, Governor Calvin Coolidge of Massachusetts." The murmuring hall suddenly resounded with a thunder of uncontrived, spontaneous applause. For the first and last time in his life Calvin Coolidge had become a symbol of revolt. The week-long frustrations of the delegates, their sense of impotence as the whip cracked, their rage at being forced through the hoops, suddenly spilled over at the mention of Coolidge's name. Quickly the nomination was seconded by the delegations of Michigan, Maryland, North Dakota, Arkansas, and Connecticut—all supposedly under senatorial control. Remmel, the old professional, knew a bandwagon when he saw one. As soon as he could get the attention of the chair, he announced that he was withdrawing his seconding of Lenroot in order to second the nomination of Coolidge. The vote was Coolidge 674½, Lenroot 146½.

On hearing the news Senator McCormick dashed back to the platform, but events had sped past him. As in Boston the previous September, an unforeseen combination of circumstances had dramatically advanced Calvin Coolidge's career, and before long another accident equally unforeseen would take him even farther. In a few confused moments in the Chicago Coliseum, in the bellowing insistence of an unknown Oregon delegate, a President had been made.

Francis Russell was a boy growing up in a Boston suburb when the police strike occurred. "It was impressed on me singularly that Halloween," he writes, "when a guardsman with rifle and bayonet pursued me through several back yards . . . I had been caught climbing an old gas streetlight and extinguishing it."

For further reading: A Puritan in Babylon, *by William Allen White (Macmillan, 1938); and* Calvin Coolidge: the Man from Vermont, *by Claude Fuess (Little, Brown, 1940).*

"A man ain't nothin' but a man"

CONTINUED FROM PAGE 37

Another question is: How superior a man would John Henry have had to be to "drive fourteen feet while the steam drill only made nine"—or even to drive the twenty feet that Neal Miller recalls? One answer might be found in the drilling contests that were popular among miners in the Rocky Mountains as reported in *The Engineering Magazine* of September, 1892. At a tournament in Helena, Montana, William Shea drove 25 5/16 inches by hand through granite in fifteen minutes. A doubles team of Davy and Tague drove 33 5/16 inches in the same time. If one man, drilling in granite, could drive more than two feet in fifteen minutes, his rate would come to eight and one half feet per hour. Two hours of drilling would put him in John Henry's class. According to Hedrick, John Henry spaced his hammering over two days. Furthermore, the red shale at Big Bend is not as hard as granite. So, clearly, the part of the tall tale of John Henry that describes the actual race is not so tall at that.

Then how tall is the account of John Henry's death? If Miller was indeed to be taken as the only eyewitness, he might know if John Henry truly laid down his hammer and died. Miller's recollection is considerably less romantic, but quite revealing of tunneling conditions as well as of the process of folk composition:

> John Henry didn't die from getting too hot in the contest with the steam drill, like you say. He drove in the heading a long time after that . . . He was killed all right, and I know the time. The boys round the tunnel told me that he was killed from a blast of rock in the heading and he was put in a box with another Negro and buried at night under the big fill at the east end of the tunnel.
>
> The bosses at the tunnel were afraid the death of John Henry would cause trouble among the Negroes, and they often got rid of dead Negroes in some way like that. All the Negroes left the tunnel once and wouldn't go in for several days. Some of them won't go in it now because they have got the notion they can still hear John Henry driving steel in there. He's a regular ghost around this place. His marks in the side of the rocks where he drove with the steam drill stayed there awhile at the east end of the tunnel but when the railroad bed was widened with double tracking they destroyed them.

If this account is true, the secret of John Henry's death was kept from the ears of John Hedrick, the woodwork foreman. He recalled that "John Henry stayed round the tunnel a year or two, then went away somewhere. I don't remember when he left . . . John Henry was there twelve months after the contest. I know. He was there when the hole was opened between shaft one and two."

So the tragic end of John Henry, if he ever lived at all to beat a steam drill down, was a piece of masterful literary embroidery.

The testimony supports the belief that a race between John Henry and a steam drill could have taken place. Although lovers of folk song fondly maintain the faith that it did, the myth is almost as important as the truth. A legend which has grown over more than half a century is itself a fact, shedding its own light. The "Ballad of John Henry" tells how a series of generations came to wish that John Henry had lived and died, whether he did or not.

For all we know, John Henry may have been a vain, hammering fool. Or perhaps, in measuring himself against a machine, he was merely doing what a foreman told him to do. In any case, judging from the testimony, he was no martyr.

But the John Henry we sing about is no mere steel driver pitted against a steam drill. He is like modern man standing in awe, in self-doubt, before the machines that progressively unman him. Tidy as the song and its ending may be, the conflict faced by John Henry in the cradle of the industrial revolution has not been resolved; it has, in fact, become vastly more troubling. As machines do still more of our work, the song seems to ask: what will become of us? Will we ever be, like the John Henry of the song, whole men again?

The tragic triumph of a fictional John Henry reassures us that man, the maker of wondrous mechanical things, is more wondrous than the things he makes; that a man who "ain't nothin' but a man" is strong and worthy of supreme dignity. The impressive thing about this simple, powerful tragedy is that while it surpasses the careful creations of many reflective poets, it has been composed collectively by numbers of men, unknown to each other and untutored in the ways of literary form. It is only a crude song, but it is also a formidable literary achievement.

Bernard Asbell is a free-lance writer, living in Connecticut, who has been a contributor to many leading magazines. In 1961, Holt, Rinehart & Winston published his best-selling book, When F. D. R. Died; *this year he is serving as President of the Society of Magazine Writers.*

The  *Parlor*

CONTINUED FROM PAGE 64

the name of a rose or the quality of a piece of ribbon or lace. Gentlemen were cautioned not to talk politics in the presence of ladies (though they often did), because in this area ladies were expected to be both uninterested and ill-informed. Religion and moral questions were to be avoided as well, for they led, according to *The Illustrated Manners Book,* "to angry, endless, and useless contests."

Ladies and gentlemen of the day were cautioned that the art of conversation was not to be taken lightly or acquired easily. It required "a cultivated mind, richly stored with a variety of useful information; a good taste; a delicate sense of propriety; a good use of language; and an easy and fluent expression." To achieve this artistic effect Harvey Newcomb, the author of *How to Be a Lady,* published in 1863, provided eleven rules, among which were: Avoid *affectation* ("it will expose you to ridicule"); Avoid *low expressions* ("a dialect peculiar to low people"); Avoid *provincialisms* ("For example, in New England, many people are in the habit of interlarding their conversation with the phrase, '*You* see.'"); Avoid *unmeaning exclamations* (such as "O my! O mercy! &c."). But the meat of all manners-manual advice about conversational decency was to avoid talking too much about one's self and one's personal problems. Late in the century the forbidden topics of polite conversation were reduced to what one elderly lady of my acquaintance used to call "The five D's": they were Dress, Diseases, Domiciles, Descendants, and Domestics. It is a great deal more difficult to discover what the mentors of manners thought *were* suitable subjects for conversation than what were not. The weather, of course, was safe. So was the opera. It was polite to enquire about a visitor's children, though even this had to be undertaken with discretion, as Miss Leslie cautioned:

> As mothers are always on the *qui vive,* (and very naturally,) be careful what you say of their children. Unless he is a decidedly handsome man, you may give offense by remarking, "The boy is the very image of his father." If the mother is a vain woman, she would much rather hear that all the children are the very image of herself. Refrain from praising too much the children of another family, particularly if the two sets of children are cousins. . . .

It was considered dangerous in the highly mobile society of America to ask questions that might remind a woman that she came from "humble" origins. It was a cliché at the turn of the century that one should not ask a prosperous San Franciscan who his grandmother was: the odds were that she had been a madam. Similarly, in the middle of the century, it was considered risky to discuss household affairs with newly rich women because "Women who have begun the world in humble life, and have been necessitated to give most of their attention to household affairs, are generally very shy in talking of housewifery, after their husbands have become rich, and are living in style, as it is called. Therefore, do not annoy them by questions on domestic economy. But converse as if they had been ladies always." There were also taboos against gossip, of course, but few women either ill- or well-bred paid much attention to them. "It is one of the greatest miseries of our life," wrote a woman who called herself "Daisy Eyebright," the author of *A Manual of Etiquette,* "that scandal is the standing dish in society, and calumny stalks abroad with perfect boldness and impunity."

The ritual of the "call" was an absolutely essential part of nineteenth-century manners, its propriety taken for granted, its uses very nearly universal. Even in the back country in the 1830's, making calls was an essential part of a woman's day. The famous British traveller Captain Frederick Marryat, visiting Detroit in 1837, when there was not "a paved street in it, or even a foot-path for a pedestrian," found that "the muddy and impassable state of the streets has given rise to a very curious system of making morning and evening calls." Detroit was then a town of many log cabins, but it was not without its proprieties. "A small one-horse cart," Marryat recorded, "is backed against the door of a house; the ladies dressed get into it, and seat themselves upon a buffalo-skin at the bottom of it; they are carried to the residence of the party upon whom they wish to call; the cart is backed in again, and they are landed dry and clean."

Books of etiquette disagreed on many details of making calls, but all agreed that they should be made. The morning call was generally a visit of about fifteen minutes; less than that was rude, more was inconsiderate of the person being called upon. "First calls" were paid on new arrivals after a "suitable" interval had been allowed them to settle their new homes. "When should a lady call first upon a new and desirable acquaintance?" asked Mrs. M. E. W. Sherwood in *Manners and Social Usages.* "Not hastily. She should have met the new and desirable acquaintance, should have been properly introduced, should feel sure that her acquaintance is desired. . . . Too much haste in making new acquaintances, however—'pushing,' as it is called—cannot be too much deprecated." It was, of course, the prerogative of the lady being called upon to decide whether she was "at home" or not. In the country, where callers might well have come some distance by carriage, it was considered rude not to be "at home" and, worse than that, to be unfriendly. But in the city it was a lady's privilege to receive callers or not, so long as she exerted discretion and was "at home" more often than not. In no city was calling more elaborate or more of a social burden than in Washington. "The American woman is making an heroic effort, here as elsewhere, to do what is expected of her," wrote the author of *Social Usages in Washington* during Theodore Roosevelt's administration. "A lady in official life sometimes devotes four afternoons in the week to the business of paying calls, making as many as thirty or even fifty in a single day." This kind of calling was merely "dropping cards" on people, an onerous task that had nothing to do with friendship or hospitality, and was merely a kind of tribute that women were expected to pay to the demons of etiquette.

The use of calling cards grew to ridiculous proportions during the nineteenth century, and the rules for using them became so elaborate that scarcely anyone could master all the nuances and idiosyncrasies. "However laughable it may appear to some persons, to see bits of pasteboard with names on them, left at the doors of houses," wrote Mrs. John Farrar early in the century, "it is a most convenient custom, and the only way of being sure that your call will be known to your friend." Mrs. Farrar, a sensible woman with humor, would have been astonished at what eventually came to be the tyranny of the card. Forty years later the anonymous author of *Social Etiquette in New York* devoted two chapters to the use of cards, one for gentlemen and one for ladies, and it was a solemn matter indeed. The discourse began:

> To the unrefined or underbred person, the visiting-card is but a trifling and insignificant bit of paper; but to the cultured disciple of social law, it conveys a subtle and unmistakable intelligence. Its texture, style of engraving, and even the hour of leaving it, combine to place the stranger whose name it bears in a pleasant or disagreeable attitude, even before his manners, conversation, and face have been able to explain his social position. The higher the civilization of a community, the more careful it is to preserve the elegance of its social forms.

Mark Twain was certainly one of "the unrefined or underbred" whom the author had in mind. Five years earlier, in *The Gilded Age,* Twain, who took special delight in needling the socially pretentious, had written of the use of cards in Washington:

> Mrs. A pays her annual visit, sits in her carriage and sends in her card with the lower right-hand corner turned down, which signifies that she has "called in person;" Mrs. B. sends down word that she is "engaged" or "wishes to be excused"—or if she is a parvenu and low-bred, she perhaps sends word that she is "not at home." Very good; Mrs. A. drives on happy and content. If Mrs. A's daughter marries, or a child is born to the family, Mrs. B. calls, sends in the card with the upper left-hand corner turned down, and then goes along about her affairs—for that inverted corner means "Congratulations." If Mrs. B.'s husband falls down stairs and breaks his neck, Mrs. A. calls, leaves her card with the upper right-hand corner turned down and then takes her departure; this corner means "Condolence." It is very necessary to get the corners right, else one may condole with a friend on a wedding or congratulate her upon a funeral. If either lady is about to leave the city, she goes to the other's house and leaves her card with "P.P.C." engraved under the name—which signifies, "Pay Parting Call."

One can almost hear the author of *Social Etiquette in New York* sneering and saying "Tsk! Tsk! Doesn't he know that P.P.C. stands for '*pour prendre congé*?' " The language of etiquette, like the decoration of the parlor, was French. In fashionable circles the "party call," which one omitted to pay on a hostess within a week of a party at the cost of social ostracism, was called a *visite de digestion.*

It was on the manners of the parlor that writers about etiquette concentrated their principal fire, though the manners of the dining room and of the street came in for their fair share of comment. The parlor was, after all, the principal private room in which public manners were most on display, and it was the place where guidance in proper behavior was presumed to be most needed.

When Frances Milton Trollope, another noted English visitor, first arrived in Cincinnati in the late 1820's she noted that "whatever may be the talents of the persons who meet together in society, the very shape, form and arrangement of the meeting is sufficient to paralyze conversation." The trouble was that the men herded together in one part of the room and the women in another (a "trouble" that is still a common

FROM *The Gibson Book,* 1907

An embarrassing interruption in the parlor was drawn by Charles Dana Gibson in 1895. The gentleman has recovered nicely, but the lady seems aware that her crushed sleeve and disarranged coiffure will give them away to the butler.

practice in many American households), and nothing seemed able to break the barrier between the sexes. Later Mrs. Trollope was surprised to discover that this segregation was equally prevalent in cities east of the Alleghenies.

The gentlemen spit, talk of elections and the price of produce, and spit again. The ladies look at each other's dresses till they know every pin by heart; talk of Parson Somebody's last sermon on the day of judgment, on Dr. T'otherbody's new pills for dyspepsia, till the "tea" is announced, when they all console themselves together for whatever they may have suffered in keeping awake, by taking more tea, coffee, hot cake and custard, hoe cake, johnny cake, waffle cake, and dodger cake, pickled peaches, and preserved cucumbers, ham, turkey, hung beef, apple sauce, and pickled oysters than were ever prepared in any other country in the known world. After this massive meal is over, they return to the drawing room, and it always appeared to me that they remained together as long as they could bear it, and then they rise *en masse,* cloak, bonnet, shawl, and exit.

In New York, where dancing was often indulged in at evening parties, James Silk Buckingham found in the 1840's that "the dancing was monotonous and indifferent; partly from languor, and partly, it is believed, from affectation of indifference, which is considered to be more genteel than vulgar vivacity." It was gentility that was taking the fun out of life, and it was gentility that continued until the end of the century to make the parlor and its amusements the kind of tribulation that leisure enforces on those who believe, as Americans did, that only work was a virtuous occupation. The functions of the parlor were social "duties" rather than friendly pleasures, and the more onerous and complicated they became, and the more silver there was to be polished, the easier it was for the American woman to justify such use of her leisure. Only among the very rich was the observance of social amenities a full-time occupation that demanded not merely extensive knowledge of the rules but the self-assurance to flout them (and make new ones) and the generalship to plan and execute the elaborate strategy of social campaigns.

For most men the parlor was one of the trials of life that one was expected to make the best of, keep a stiff upper lip about, and try not to make a fool of oneself in. It was part of the sacrifice that the American male grudgingly granted was due his wife. To children the parlor was, of course, a place where they were to be seen and not heard, except when their mothers asked them to perform a newly learned piece on the piano for the benefit of a lady who sat stiffly with her gloved hands folded in her lap, or to show off a few French phrases they had just learned at school. They might "speak when spoken to," but if they ventured to speak on their own, they were hustled from the room. Even the parlor games which children had enjoyed in the early part of the century became obsolete. To the lady of the house the parlor was, or was supposed to be, the expression of her refinement and the stage on which she displayed her breeding, her bibelots, her poise, and her culture.

The downfall of a room which placed such a burden on so many members of the family was bound to come sooner or later, in form if not entirely in substance. Many of the parlor's social values were false, and its discomforts far outweighed its pleasures or even the returns it brought in social prestige. Moreover, its proprieties were so blown up as to menace the best qualities of frank and casual republican manners and hospitality. As America grew in power and importance and became less self-conscious about its cultural shortcomings, it felt less and less need to look over its shoulder to Europe for its standards of polite behavior.

Practical as well as cultural considerations helped restore a degree of balance as the nineteenth century drew to a close. For one thing, more and more people were living in cities, and a smaller and smaller percentage of city families were living in houses. In the East, by the 1870's, the value of urban land had made the cost of building a "town house" prohibitive except to the rich, and as a result the apartment house began to appear. Only in expensive apartments was there a room that could be shut off exclusively for formal use, and the parlor became the sitting room for all of the family every day. Its furniture became more comfortable, its atmosphere more relaxed; the children were allowed to do their homework at the center table under a gas fixture which shed its blue-white light from a ceiling chandelier. Even in large houses and expensive apartments the word "parlor," identified with the parvenu wealth of the earlier part of the century, lost caste; now decorated with antiques imported from England and France and Italy rather than with American-made furniture, the parlor became the "drawing room."

But the parlor did not die quietly all at once and without a prolonged whimper. It had to be beaten to death with words, some of them indignant and some humorous. The attacks on the extravagance of the parlor, its size as compared with other rooms in the house, and its status as a sort of family museum only for special use started early in the century. By the 1870's the Victorian parlor began to give way to the "artistic" parlor which gloried in the quaint and the exotic. Cozy corners and Turkish nooks, piled with cushions and decorated with cattails and peacock feathers, with brass pots and taborets inlaid with mother-of-pearl,

Cornhill's Magazine, 1861; CULVER PICTURES

Even an elegant English "drawing room," which the plain American parlor sought to emulate in the late nineteenth century, could be a scene of social discomfort, as this British satirical drawing shows. The dinner guests have just finished their meal, and the evening guests are arriving, hats in hand; the pleasant mixture the hostess is hoping for has not yet jelled.

drove out formality and ushered in romantic notions. One writer on the home called it "Yankee rococo," but whatever it was it combined clutter with comfort and substituted polite sensuousness for the straight-spined piety of a few decades before. People looked back with few regrets at the time when the parlor was a "temple of form and fidgetiness," when "the children were watched with lynx eyes lest they should displace or soil something," and when the entertainment of friends was a social discipline. Even the manners books relaxed in their attitudes, and though they continued to give advice on every conceivable aspect of social deportment, they no longer thought it essential for a young man when he married to get rid of all his bachelor acquaintances lest his bride find them unsuitable to invite into her parlor.

But such habits of mind as the parlor represented are not easily shaken, nor are objects once thought beautiful or special or associated with times of happiness or tragedy quickly cast aside for the new and fashionable. One does not have to look far today in nearly any part of the country for a parlor in which at least the echoes of a century ago are still alive. There are still, after all, a great many men and women whose childhood was lived in the late Victorian era; in their houses the television set now sits next to a whatnot and the radio is planted on a rosewood table with carved and twisted legs. Their forebears still watch them from gilt frames and they still cherish their green-shaded student lamps, long since wired for electricity. Fashions in decorating are continually nudging each other out of the way, but manners have a way of persisting, and people whose manners were tempered in the fire of the parlor are as dignified as they ever were.

"We are fast becoming a parlorless nation," wrote Lillian Hart Tryon nearly fifty years ago. "The accidental limitations of space and of service in modern life, and the increased expenses of buildings, as well as the noble intention of simplifying the house, have contributed to the result . . . The parlor now is relegated to the cold and viewless side [of the house], or is crowded into a corner of the hall, with two chairs and a palm. We could not get our parlors back if we tried, because we ourselves have changed . . . Life is too full to have patience with formalities. The cry of the time is for few friends and good ones." But even more important than the shrinking house, its mechanization, and the shortage of service was the change that had gradually come over women. As the century turned they began to view the world differently, and to stride through it with a quickened pace.

The parlor had been not only the forum over which women presided but, except for the militant feminists, almost the only arena in which they faced the world outside their homes. When Harriet Martineau visited America in the 1840's she had found only seven kinds of employment open to women—teaching, needlework, keeping boarders, working in cotton mills, typesetting, book-binding, and domestic service. Of these only teaching and, possibly, keeping boarders were considered respectable occupations for ladies. Toward the end of the century came a shift of heart and of opportunity. The professions of law, medicine, and architecture grudgingly opened their doors, if only a crack; offices wooed women to run the newfangled typewriter; the reputation of Florence Nightingale had made nursing honorable, and even being an actress was not considered as entirely disreputable as it had been only a few years before. Colleges like Vassar, Holyoke, Smith, and Bryn Mawr were determined to give women an education not only equivalent to that given to men but of precisely the same sort. All these developments had begun to make women impatient with the drudgery of housekeeping and the finicky world of the parlor. ("Only our failures marry," said the militantly intellectual Miss M. Carey Thomas, first president of Bryn Mawr.)

The American woman was moving again. In the early years of the century she had followed her husband west over the mountains or along the still waters of the Erie Canal to the forests and the prairie, toting her chattels and as many symbols of civilization as her man and his wagon could manage. She had disappeared into the unfamiliar and the lonely, into the relentless winds of wide horizons or the stillness of trees. But by the end of the century she was moving into an entirely different world, a world made by men for men, a world of facts and figures, of eyeshades and roll-top desks, of buck passing and ledgers and letter presses. But it was a world as filled with adventure and with as many unfamiliar kinds of weariness, drudgery, and boredom as the wilderness had imposed on her mother a generation before.

But this time her dream house was not built around a parlor—elegant, formal, sweet-smelling, and immaculate, a place to sit with your ankles neatly together; now she wanted a place where you could put your feet up, a place to stretch out, not a place to sit bolt upright clutching a tea cup. It took a feminist revolution to make women see that there was some sense in men's attitude toward the parlor after all.

The foregoing article is adapted from a chapter in The Domesticated Americans, *by Russell Lynes, just published by Harper & Row. Mr. Lynes, managing editor of* Harper's Magazine, *author of many books and of several contributions to* AMERICAN HERITAGE, *recently became a member of the Landmarks Preservation Commission, an arm of the New York City government.*

Nature's God and the Founding Fathers

CONTINUED FROM PAGE 7

tion. He wished his tombstone to cite him in three capacities only: "Author of the Declaration of American Independence; of the Statute of Virginia for Religious Freedom; and Father of the University of Virginia." The order was chronological, but in a most important sense the three accomplishments were one and indivisible. The Declaration of Independence envisaged a free society ruled by consent of the governed. But informed decision and consent could be based only on good public education; and good education, in turn, could be based only on complete freedom of the mind. In the history of the new republic the first fundamental challenge to freedom of the mind came in the area of religion.

It is a curious fact of American history that the man who was inseparably associated with Jefferson in his fight for religious freedom, and who was to become his closest friend for nearly half a century, grew up only thirty-odd miles from Monticello, yet never met him until late in 1776. James Madison of Montpelier, in Port Conway, Virginia, came to the capitol at Williamsburg in May of that year, an elected delegate to the state convention. By that time, Jefferson was off to his appointment with fame in Philadelphia, and so the two did not meet until the following autumn—and even then their contact was slight. But in the meantime something had happened at Williamsburg to form a bond between them no less strong for its resting temporarily unperceived.

The government of Virginia was in process of being overhauled in the spring of 1776, and although young Madison, a relatively unknown delegate, did not have a great deal to do with the new state constitution, he was a member of a committee appointed to draw up a bill of rights. The great George Mason of Gunston Hall was chief author of the articles in this bill, which was to become the prototype for similar manifestoes in other states as well as, eventually, for the Bill of Rights of the United States Constitution.

It must have cheered Jefferson to see that prominent among the Virginia articles was one on religious freedom. Madison was instrumental in giving that article its final and significant form when the committee proposal went before the Virginia convention on June 12, 1776. Only five years out of college at Princeton, he was already an accomplished student of constitutional law, a man cast very much in Jefferson's mold. As he saw it, Mason's expression of the principle of religious freedom was deficient in two respects: it allowed for continuation of a state-supported church, and it spoke of "toleration in the exercise of religion" rather than absolute freedom of conscience. Recognizing that it was not quite time to push for disestablishment in Virginia, Madison let that go, but proposed a rewording that would move forward from the idea of mere toleration (which implied the right of the state either to grant or withhold religious freedom) to that of freedom of conscience as an unalienable natural right. The convention was not willing to go quite that far, but, in its permanent form, the article pronounced that "all men are equally entitled to the free exercise of religion, according to the dictates of conscience." It was a quiet yet important triumph in the struggle for complete liberty of thought in America.

When he began to become well acquainted with Madison, in the summer of 1779, Jefferson was fresh from a half-successful effort to abolish state sanction of religion in Virginia. Government salaries for Anglican ministers had been suspended, but their church was still functioning as the official one in the state, and other impediments to religious liberty persisted. It was impossible to be legally married, for example, unless the ceremony was performed by an Anglican clergyman, and heresy against the Christian faith was still a crime. Jefferson's comprehensive "Bill for Establishing Religious Freedom" would have swept aside all such restrictions, as well as forbidding government support of any church. But it ran into fierce opposition in the Virginia legislature when it was introduced in June, 1779, and failed to pass.

Nevertheless, the Bill for Religious Freedom must have exerted a strong attractive force between Jefferson and Madison. They were now often in close consultation, Jefferson as newly elected governor, Madison as a member of his executive council; their personal friendship was also growing fast. Although Madison had been, from his college days, more skeptical and less orthodox than he has been painted by many biographers, his commitment to absolute freedom of thought as the undergirding of a free society was henceforth more intense. By the time Jefferson left for France, Madison was well prepared to carry on their campaign not only in Virginia, but in the first Congress, to which he would go as a representative in 1789.

Washington praying at Valley Forge, a favorite but apocryphal story, was commemorated in a United States stamp.

In Virginia, Madison's skill finally brought victory for Jefferson's disestablishment bill, but not without a tough running battle against an opposition headed by the redoubtable Patrick Henry. By 1784 the state Anglican hierarchy was vociferously pressing for new tax funds to support the church, and Henry proposed an annual assessment for "the support of the Christian religion or of some Christian church," without naming any particular sect. This attempted shift from the traditional, single-church form of establishment to the multiple, embracing several denominations, was part of a trend now apparent in more than one of the states of the new nation. It was a type of defensive strategy which would continue for nearly two centuries, as efforts to retain government sanction for religion moved to an ever broader and less sectarian base. In Virginia in 1784 the Presbyterians, hitherto enemies of establishment, now joined the phalanx demanding it in the broader form. They seemed as ready, Madison noted to his friend James Monroe, "to set up an establishment which is to take them in as they were to pull down that which shut them out."

Meanwhile, Madison was by no means impotent on the other side of the issue. He anonymously wrote his now famous "Memorial and Remonstrance Against Religious Assessments" (1785), which was circulated wide and far in Virginia as a petition to which thousands signed their names in protest against the renewed prospect of religious establishment. As copy after copy of the petition, crowded with signatures, streamed into the Virginia Assembly, it became very clear that the majority of the people were in no mood to forsake the religious freedom they had been promised by the 1776 Declaration of Rights. The surprised proponents of the assessment bill never even bothered to bring it to a vote.

Madison's "Remonstrance" was a piece of shrewd political propaganda. It struck a chord more in harmony with the orthodox Christianity of those to whom it was addressed than his private views might have sustained, yet it echoed the rationalist strain of his religious discussions with Jefferson.

In fifteen paragraphs, many of them harking back to the popular article on religion in the 1776 Declaration of Rights, he argued against government support of the church. Every man's religion, he wrote, must be left to the conviction and conscience of every man; and it is the right of every man to exercise it as these may dictate. This right is in its nature an unalienable right . . . because the opinions of men, depending only on the evidence contemplated by their own minds, cannot follow the dictates of other men. . . . We maintain therefore that in matters of Religion, no man's right is abridged by the institution of Civil Society, and that Religion is wholly exempt from its cognizance. . . . Who does not see that the same authority which can establish Christianity, in exclusion of all other Religions, may establish with the same ease any particular sect of Christians, in exclusion of all other Sects? . . . Whilst we assert for ourselves a freedom to embrace, to profess, and to observe the Religion which we believe to be of divine origin, we cannot deny an equal freedom to those whose minds have not yet yielded to the evidence which has convinced us. . . .

It is noteworthy, since it bears on the meaning of the First Amendment to the Constitution, that to Madison and the thousands of Virginians who signed his petition, "establishment of religion" meant any government sponsorship of any or all religions, and not just the European pattern of an exclusive, official state church. (The "Remonstrance" refers repeatedly to Henry's general assessment bill as "the proposed establishment.") They wanted a solid "wall of separation between church and state," to use a phrase Jefferson invented later. Acting on the theory that a good time to dispatch an enemy was when he was on the run, Madison and his friends in the legislature now took Jefferson's Bill for Religious Liberty off the shelf where it had seasoned since 1779, and this time saw it voted in by a substantial majority. In principle it was a twin to Madison's "Remonstrance," but even more trenchant in its rhetoric and forthright in its defense of absolute freedom of thought and expression —a forerunner, as well as, in a sense, an interpretation of the First Amendment to the Constitution.

A last-minute effort by the opposition to confine the benefits of the law to Christians instead of protecting even (as Jefferson noted) "the Infidel of every denomination," failed. Early in 1786, Madison was able to send his friend the news that through their collaboration the most sweeping guarantee of freedom of conscience in the history of the western world had become a statute of Virginia. He felt that its provisions, he wrote Jefferson, "have in this country extinguished forever the ambitious hope of making laws for the human mind." Fervently sharing this senti-

NEW-YORK HISTORICAL SOCIETY

This political cartoon of 1807 spared nothing in contrasting President Jefferson with Washington, already venerated as "the Father of his Country." Not only is Jefferson associated with vile animals and "infidel" authors, but his lamp of knowledge pours out fumes and smoke, and he himself looks slightly dissolute, presumably from loose and godless living.

ment, Jefferson saw to it that the new statute was translated into French and Italian, widely published, and "inserted in the new Encyclopedie." He reported "infinite approbation in Europe."

The example of Virginia—by far the largest of the thirteen states in population, and home of a cluster of distinguished men headed by the revered Washington—could hardly be ignored in the rest of America. The winds of revolution already had blown away much restrictive custom and legislation by 1786. Most of the other states had recently passed bills of rights honoring religious freedom, even though, with the exception of Rhode Island, New Jersey, and New York, they still had church establishment in at least the multiple form, embracing several sects. It was to be a number of years before any of them matched Virginia, yet it was natural that her action greatly strengthened the general current toward increased freedom of thought and an accompanying separation of church and state.

But it was to be almost by accident that the question of religious freedom first arose at the national level. The Constitutional Convention, gathering at Philadelphia in the spring of 1787, ignored it for many weeks—not because it was felt to be unimportant, but because it was considered the business of the states rather than of the central government. But as a hot August steamed into a hot September, it became obvious that the federal machinery designed by men like Madison, Alexander Hamilton, and Roger Sherman was far more powerful than the old Articles of Confederation. What about the rights of the people under such a government? They ought to be, asserted George Mason, "the pole star of political conduct." The state governments were, in 1787, the guardians of those rights; but the new Constitution greatly reduced the power of the states. With Mason at the center, a small nucleus of delegates began to agitate for specific guarantees, to be built into the Constitution itself. Charles Pinckney, of South Carolina, urged a ban on religious tests for federal officeholders, and the Convention—thinking, no doubt, of their own wide spread of religious opinion—quickly adopted it (Article VI).

Still, the movement for a full bill of rights, similar to those prevailing in a majority of the states, found little support. Mason was deeply disturbed, and announced that he would "sooner chop off his right hand than put it to the Constitution as it now stands." But Roger Sherman expressed the more general feeling when he said that "the State Declarations of Rights are not repealed by this Constitution; and being in force are sufficient." The tired delegates brought the Convention to a close on September 17, 1787, and the Constitution was submitted to the states without a bill of rights. Mason did not chop off his hand, but he did quit the Convention without signing.

As the contest over ratification swung back and forth in the various state legislatures during 1787–88, the federalists were forced to admit that a compromise was in order. From New England to Georgia there was intense pressure for a national bill of rights as a condition of ratification. Some federalists at first viewed this as nothing but camouflage for an attempt to frustrate ratification altogether. Alexander Hamilton was angry and contemptuous. It was the plan of the antifederalists, he declared, "to frighten the people with ideal bugbears, in order to mould them to their own purposes. The unceasing cry of these designing croakers is, My friends, your liberty is invaded!" Washington, choosing somewhat milder language, was inclined to agree.

There doubtless was some basis for this opinion; yet it became more and more difficult to hold it unequivocally. Pamphlets and newspaper articles sprouted on both sides of the question, but the antifederalist clamor for a bill of rights clearly had a grass-roots origin. The issue of religious freedom, while not at this time an agitated question, drew some attention. As a committee of Baptist leaders in Virginia saw it, the new Constitution did not make "sufficient provision for the secure enjoyment of religious liberty"; and an imaginative antifederalist writer in Massachusetts complained that although there was no guarantee of freedom of conscience for the people, the ban on religious tests might result in the election of a Mohammedan President.

Concern over individual liberty, of course, was by no means the exclusive property of antifederalists. Indeed, there were many on the other side (including Madison and Jefferson, both of whom must be counted as federalists at this early stage) who were as deeply devoted to liberty as anyone in the antifederalist ranks. Madison had been somewhat wary of a federal bill of rights for fear that specifying what the central government might *not* infringe would imply that it could suppress other rights, not enumerated. But reconsideration plus advice from Jefferson changed his mind; and numerous other important federalists finally conceded the expedience if not the need of such a bill. The upshot was that as the state conventions one by one ratified the Constitution, most of them did so with a strong recommendation for the addition of protective amendments. Madison found himself, in March of 1789, setting out from Virginia as a representative to the First Congress, pledged to introduce a large batch of amendments. Among them were, in substance, the ten that now make up the Bill of Rights.

With long congressional debates developing over such urgent matters as new revenue laws, and such intriguing ones as whether the Chief Executive should be called "His Highness" or just "the President," it was June before Madison was able to get any action on the proposed amendments. Even then there was some reluctance to discuss a national bill of rights in preference to questions of greater sectional interest, and he was obliged to lecture his House colleagues on what their constituents expected of them—particularly "those safeguards which they have been long accustomed to have interposed between them and the magistrate who exercises the sovereign power." He then presented his list of amendments and gave a long speech defending them. One prophetic point he made was in the form of a quotation from Jefferson saying that the federal courts would "consider themselves in a peculiar manner the guardians of those rights" stipulated in such amendments to the Constitution.

The congressional history of Madison's amendment on religion throws some interesting illumination on the question of just what it meant in its final form, when after much rewording it became part of the First Amendment. He first introduced it as, "The civil rights of none shall be abridged on account of religious belief or worship, nor shall any national religion be established, nor shall the full and equal rights of conscience be in any manner, or on any pretext, abridged." Against the background of the Jefferson-Madison view of religion in its relation to democratic government, the emphasis here is unmistakable. It goes straight to what they conceived to be the heart of the matter: absolute freedom of thought for the individual citizen without government pressure toward any system of belief whatever. It seems likely that, had Madison's original wording been adopted, official sanction for even the vague theism suggested by the motto first engraved on United States coins in 1864 ("In God We Trust"), or by the interpolation in 1954 of "under God" in the national oath of allegiance, would have been considered unconstitutional. (Both resulted from acts of Congress.) Certainly his wording would have buttressed the recent Supreme Court decision against the devotional use of prayers or Bible reading in public schools. Whether it would have thrown light on other controversial church-state issues—for example the payment of chaplains for service in the armed forces—is more problematical.

There is no doubt, however, where Madison and Jefferson stood when it came to practical applications. They were meticulous. In 1789 Madison opposed (unsuccessfully) the appointment of official chaplains for Congress because "these are to be paid out of the national taxes"; and Jefferson, as President, refused to follow the practice of Washington and Adams in proclaiming certain days for religious observance ("I do not believe," he explained, "it is for the interest of religion to invite the civil magistrate to direct its exercises, its discipline, or its doctrines. . . . Fasting and prayer are religious exercises; the enjoining them an act of discipline . . ."). To Madison and Jefferson and their followers the word "establish" meant what it had in Virginia: any government support, by taxation or otherwise, of any religious program.

Madison's original amendment on religion, however, was soon altered. It was referred to a committee of which he was vice-chairman, and evidently caused much discussion—although no exact committee records, unfortunately, were kept. On August 15, 1789, the House as a whole took up the question, considering it in a shorter and less explicit form ("No religion shall be established by law, nor shall the equal rights of conscience be infringed"). Although this wording was less forthright, some members were apprehensive of its effect: Peter Silvester, of New York, said that he "feared it might be thought to have a tendency to abolish religion altogether." The amendment was sent forward to the Senate as, "Congress shall make no law establishing religion, or to prevent the free exercise thereof, or to infringe the rights of conscience." There can be little question that the phrase "or to prevent the free exercise thereof" indicated a desire that the prohibition against establishment should not be interpreted as hostile to religion. The conventional forms of Christianity were still overwhelmingly in use in America, despite significant inroads by deism.

As for Madison, his own sharp focus on utter freedom of thought and expression as the essence of what is now the First Amendment is shown by his introduction, at this time, of an additional amendment specifically forbidding any state to infringe the rights of conscience, freedom of speech, and a free press. This addition was, he thought, "the most valuable on the whole list." Somewhat surprisingly (in view of the antifederalist feeling against domination of the states by the central government), it was sustained by the House, and went to the Senate together with the article on religion and fifteen other amendments.

The twenty-two members of the Senate, which in general was more conservative than the House of Representatives, combined some of the House amendments and dropped others, including Madison's "most valuable" one. Nevertheless, they rejected several motions to amend the House statement on religion to make it prohibit government support of "any particular denomination of religion in preference to another." This was important, for it implied that their intent was to

LIBRARY OF CONGRESS

The idea of full separation of church and state is graphically suggested in Thomas Nast's nineteenth-century cartoon. The goddess of liberty demurely declines to favor any sect whatsoever with admission beyond the portals of government.

impose a neutral policy on the government with respect to religion in general—not merely to prevent one sect from gaining government favor at the expense of others. Such an intent was suggested further in the rewording arrived at by the Senate on September 9: "Congress shall make no law establishing articles of faith, or a mode of worship, or prohibiting the free exercise of religion." Here the emphasis of "establish" leans toward the idea of government infringement on "the rights of conscience"—even though that phrase was dropped from the House version. The potential application to such matters as public school prayers, for instance, seems obvious.

Yet it was not clear that the Senate's version of the religion clause prohibited tax support, and perhaps for that reason the House refused to accept the revision. A joint committee, with Madison as chairman of the three House members and Oliver Ellsworth of Connecticut as his counterpart for the Senate, then considered the difficulty—again without leaving us minutes of their discussion—and came up with the wording that has become part of the First Amendment: "Congress shall make no law respecting an establishment of religion, or prohibiting the free exercise thereof." Madison could not have been pleased to see the key phrase about "the rights of conscience" abandoned—for him that clarified the basic intent of the amendment—but he was convinced that in its final form the first article of the Bill of Rights could be reasonably interpreted as prohibiting federal support of religious activities in any form.

That, as has been noted, was the way he and Jefferson interpreted it during their terms as President, and for the rest of their lives. At the same time, both of them realized that while they had led a successful campaign for separation of church and state as an essential footing in the structure of democracy, their theoretical reasons for doing so were grasped by relatively few of their countrymen. They knew their ideal was still remote: a society so free that its only ideological commitment would be to freedom of the mind. Much of the support they had been able to rally for a barrier between church and state had other sources. True, it sprang in part from a native intellectual current against absolutism which has never failed to flow in America despite counteracting currents of great force. But in part it came from the mutual and competitive mistrust of the various religious sects toward one another. Always pragmatic, Jefferson and Madison saw the value of this, despite their own rejection of revealed religion. Variety of belief was a useful insurance against tyranny.

The history of the First Amendment since 1791, when the last of the necessary eleven states ratified the federal Bill of Rights, has been one of fluctuating interpretation. This has been most notable during the last fifty years, during which, for the most part, the Supreme Court has found that the Fourteenth Amendment enjoins the guarantees of the First upon the states, for the protection of every citizen. There has been some confusion and inconsistency: schoolchildren swear allegiance to one nation "under God," yet cannot be led in official school prayers, however nondenominational. Over a period of years, however, the trend of Court decisions has been toward strict separation of church and state, in a manner that assuredly would please Jefferson and Madison if they were here to see it. Indeed, the Justices have shown a strong penchant for citing these champions of freedom in explaining and supporting recent Court decisions.

There is nothing sacred about the reasoning of any of our ancestors, on this or any other matter. But whether one agrees with Jefferson and Madison or not, with regard to how high and impassable the wall between church and state ought to stand in a free society, they deserve to be remembered and understood, as the two among the Founding Fathers who devoted more of their minds and lives to this great problem than anyone else. They were an intellectual *avant-garde* whose probing of the relationship between religion and democracy went beyond the more or less traditional attitudes of most Americans between 1776 and 1791. Yet they were the center of a high-pressure area in the climate of opinion of their time, and their conclusions were strongly reflected in the Constitution as it finally was adopted.

Their thinking, moreover, can be fairly understood only as emerging from the matrix of the Enlightenment, of which—with such men as Benjamin Franklin, Thomas Paine, James Monroe, and even George Washington and John Adams—they were indubitably the intellectual offspring. The impact of "natural religion" on the genesis of democratic liberty, through their influence, has too often been ignored.

Writing to Dr. Benjamin Rush in 1800, shortly before he became President, Jefferson alleged certain clerical "schemes" to breach the religion clause of the First Amendment. He would oppose them with all his power, he said, "for I have sworn upon the altar of God eternal hostility against every form of tyranny over the mind of man." It was "Nature's God" that he was thinking of; and for that vow above all others the altar was not to be found, he believed, within the limits of any dogmatic creed.

For further reading: Church and State in the United States, *by Anson P. Stokes (Harper, 1950);* The Birth of the Bill of Rights, *by Robert A. Rutland (Collier Books, 1962).*

"Old Abe" the Battle Eagle

CONTINUED FROM PAGE 33

reception was less happy. This was late in 1861, and St. Louis contained a mixed population, partly Unionist and partly Confederate in its sympathies. The 8th Wisconsin at this time wore gray uniforms—in those early days of the war many Northern regiments were attired in what was already being recognized as Confederate gray, since uniforms then were provided by the state authorities, who were not always up-to-date on army regulations—and in St. Louis the secessionists cheered and the Unionists jeered, which was not at all the way to greet a good Union regiment. People even threw things at the soldiers, someone on the sidewalk called Abe a buzzard, and in the excitement he broke his cord and flew up to a chimney top, from which it took the Wisconsin boys a good half hour to recover him. It was argued that Abe had understood and resented the "buzzard" insult.

Legends began to form about this unusual mascot, and they are embalmed in a sprightly book called *The Eagle Regiment,* which an anonymous regimental historian produced in 1890, when memories had perhaps grown slightly hazy. It was asserted that in St. Louis, despite the people who jeered, the regiment received, and firmly rejected, an offer of $500 for Old Abe. It was also said that the regiment had another mascot, a small dog named Frank, who became such a pal of the eagle that it would catch rabbits and squirrels for the bird to eat, the friendship turning, at last, to bitter enmity when Old Abe, on short rations, tried to eat Frank himself. It was related, doubtless with much truth, that in camp Old Abe was something of a nuisance. He had long since grown so well adjusted to military life that his tether had been discarded, and he got into everything, tipping over pails of water, snatching any rations that were left around, and now and then, just for fun, tearing up clothing that had been washed and hung out to dry. Foragers who came in with poultry requisitioned from secessionist chicken coops never dared leave the loot unguarded. Old Abe would get it, every time.

Abe made a friend out of the soldier who carried him. He got his drinking water by tipping his head back and letting the soldier pour water down his throat from a canteen. On occasion he would shake hands (as it was called) with this man, taking the soldier's finger in his beak and chuckling hoarsely as he pretended to bite it. The bearer insisted that Abe had an elephant's memory; if anyone teased him he would remember it and would attack his tormentor the next time they met, even if it was weeks later. No soldier not a member of the 8th Wisconsin, it was said, could come near him.

By the regulations Old Abe was not supposed to be taken into battle, and when action began he was left in camp. There were times, however, when he got under fire, and the men told tall stories about this. In an engagement at Farmington, Mississippi, it was said, Old Abe's perch was lugged up to the firing line. Bullets were coming in pretty thick, and the soldiers were ordered to lie down—whereat Abe got off his perch and crouched low on the grass, flapping back up to the crossbar as soon as the men stood up to advance. It was also said that he went all through the hot battle of Corinth, Mississippi, in the fall of 1862, screaming and flapping his wings when the men cheered. It was in this battle that he left his position, soaring up over the battle and coming down at last on the extreme left of the regiment, where his bearer recovered him.

The stories about this eagle's conduct under fire may have gained something in the postwar years, but they were devoutly believed by the veterans. It was insisted that in action Old Abe, wreathed in smoke, would peer up and down the line, as if trying to see how things were going. Sharp musket fire seemed to depress him, but the heavy thump-bump of artillery fire stimulated him; he would stand erect, screaming and flapping his wings. Now and then, when things were especially hot, he would give a series of five or six especially shrill screams, ending in a startling trill which (as the veracious regimental historian declared) "was perfectly inspiring to the soldiers."

He had a sort of vocabulary, which got full play when there was no fighting going on. When surprised by anything, he would give a wild whistle. When he knew he was about to eat he would chuckle gleefully; when he recognized an old friend he would give vent to a delicate little coo, almost like a dove. When rations were short he would utter a complaining whine. His bearer was officially detailed to forage liberally for him on the surrounding countryside; all in all, Old Abe seems to have fared pretty well.

During the Vicksburg campaign, the 8th Wisconsin was formed on parade one day for inspection by Generals Ulysses S. Grant and William Tecumseh Sherman. Old Abe was on his perch, and when the men cheered their generals he flapped and screamed, and both generals doffed their hats to him in response.

Old Abe reached his full manhood, or eaglehood, apparently just about the time his army career came to an end. In the summer of 1864 the 8th Wisconsin "veteranized"—that is, a majority of the men signed up for another three-year hitch, those who refused to re-enlist being known as "non-veterans." That fall the non-veterans were sent back home, their time having expired, and they took Old Abe with them; at which point the feathers on his head and neck turned white, so that the men called him their "baldheaded veteran."

At Madison, Wisconsin, Old Abe was formally presented to the governor of the state. He was officially given quarters in a basement room of the state capitol, and in good weather he had the run of Capitol Park.

Now began his career as distinguished veteran. He was lugged off to the Republican convention in 1868 which nominated Grant for the Presidency, and no old soldiers' reunion in Wisconsin was complete without him. He went to the huge national encampment of the Grand Army of the Republic, at Chicago, in 1875, and the next year the state legislature voted funds to send him to the Philadelphia Exposition. Meanwhile, he lived in state in his basement room. Whenever a former eagle-bearer from the old regiment came in (there had been six of them, altogether) Old Abe (on the word of the regimental historian) would recognize him, rubbing his head against the man's cheek and gurgling and clucking with pleasure.

His end came in 1881, when there was a minor fire in the capitol basement which produced great clouds of smoke. This bird who had breathed smoke on the battlefields got a little too much of it this time, and it suffocated him. He had had a twenty-year career, and there never was an American eagle like him . . . on the word of the 8th Wisconsin, veteran volunteers.

READING, WRITING, AND HISTORY

By BRUCE CATTON

The Year of Change

The United States is always turning a corner. Nothing ever quite stays fixed. No matter what period you select for examination, it always seems to be a moment of transition, when one age is giving way to another. Although it is the common fate of mankind to feel that the golden age lies somewhere in the past, in this country we forever appear to be just leaving the golden age; it is the time we ourselves knew, bafflingly changing its character just when we had concluded that it was permanent; and if we are compelled to brood about the future it is because the future is always beginning to take shape before our eyes.

One of the greatest moments of change, obviously, came somewhere in the middle of the second decade of the twentieth century. Ordinarily we ascribe the profound change which then began to the First World War, which knocked the props out from under so much of Western society. Yet the war itself may have been the product of change rather than its cause. Perhaps the transformation had already commenced when the rulers of Europe made their fateful, ruinous decision in the early summer of 1914.

Paul Angle is a man who thinks this is so. As director of the Chicago Historical Society he has just finished an eighteen-year stint of examining every page of the Chicago *Tribune* for the period from 1895 through 1913, supplementing this with an equally thorough study of such magazines as *The Independent, The Nation,* the *Literary Digest, The Outlook,* the *Century,* and the *Ladies' Home Journal;* topping off with careful perusal of such items as the *World Almanac, Spalding's Official Baseball Guide,* and two standard biographies of Woodrow Wilson. This study has led him to two conclusions—first, that that period was an authentic golden age of a sort, and, second, that it came to an end and gave way to a different age before the great war in Europe ever began.

He sets forth his argument persuasively:

> Consider, if you will, the income tax, and the changes, social and economic, which it effected. Consider the New Freedom with its shift of emphasis in the goals of government. Consider the coming of age of the automobile and the evidence it offered of the perfection of mass production. Consider the beginnings of automation, bearing then the lowly term of labor saving. Consider the acceleration of the suffrage and prohibition movements. Consider the revolution in women's dress and the increasing frankness in drama and fiction. And consider the impact of "modern" art and "modern" music. I hold that after 1913 life in the United States would have changed radically even if there had been no World War.

What, specifically, was life in 1913 changing *from*?

In 1913 the United States was still predominantly a rural nation. More than half of all the people lived either on farms or in towns of fewer than 2,500 inhabitants; we were still, basically, a nation of small-towners. Yet the change was well under way. During the first ten years of the new century the urban population had increased by thirty-four per cent, while the rural population had gone up by only eleven per cent. Furthermore, the immense shift in the weight of population had begun. The Pacific Coast area was even then the most rapidly growing section of the entire country; although California in 1913 still ranked no better than twelfth in population among the states of the Union, the trend that would bring it up to the top in another half century was there to see if anyone had had an eye for it.

Along with this there was, equally visible and equally fateful, the development of the automobile industry. New York's annual Automobile Show in January of 1913 found eighty-eight manufacturers putting more than 700 vehicles on display, at prices ranging from $395 up to $7,000; the angular, blocky cars of earlier days were beginning to be streamlined, the electric starter was coming into use, and the automobile was becoming something the ordinary man or woman could handle.

Crossroads: 1913, by Paul M. Angle. Rand, McNally & Company. 278 pp. $5.95.

Furthermore, the business was expanding beyond anything that anyone—except, probably, Henry Ford—had ever thought possible. By the end of 1913 more than 1,190,000 passenger cars were registered, a number which seems small enough today but which was fantastic by the standards of the day. (In 1900 there were just 8,000 cars.) Even more significant was the rate of growth. Nearly half of all of those cars, 461,500, were produced in 1913 alone.

Production of auto trucks, incidentally, lagged far behind. In all the United States there were in 1913 fewer than 68,000 trucks, and the *World Almanac* remarked that "there is nothing to indicate that this branch of the industry will ever progress as has the passenger car division." Still, the truck did seem to have possibilities. Considering the potentialities of "the auto wagon," the Chicago *Tribune* said whimsically that "highly imaginative men have indulged themselves with fanciful expectations of the horseless city." In Chicago alone, more than five million tons of merchandise were transported by truck in 1912.

Politics was changing. Woodrow Wilson had become President, had broken precedent of long standing by going to Congress in person to read his messages, and was driving ahead toward a vast, epoch-making extension of the federal government's powers over the nation's economic life. In his inaugural address he warned that "we have not counted the human cost of our industrial achievements" and declared that "the government has been used too often for private and selfish purposes." Government must concern itself with things previously left in other hands: specifically, there needed to be tariff reform, a new banking and currency system . . .

Out of which there came the Federal Reserve System, devised, in Wilson's words, "so that banks may be the instruments, not the masters, of business and of individual enterprise and initiative." Out of which, also, there came the income tax: mild enough, in all conscience, by present-day standards—it came in originally as part of the tariff bill, and it was devised to make up for the loss in revenue which would come from lower tariff rates—it imposed a "normal" tax of one per cent on incomes above $4,000, with additional surtaxes ranging up to three per cent on incomes over $100,000. Not very many people in the America of that day had incomes of more than $4,000. The burden was light, and the step was popular. Yet as liberal a magazine as *The Nation* warned that there was no theoretical limit to the income tax, and pointed out that "it is possible for governments to increase repeatedly the rate of such a tax, without being stopped by its sudden non-productiveness."

Mr. Angle ranges far and wide in his examination of the year of transition, discussing everything from women's dress, which seemed, to the conservative, dismayingly provocative, to the new dances (tango, maxixe, bunny hug, and turkey trot), which seemed even worse; touching on the rising motion-picture industry, the burgeoning of "ragtime," the appearance of such composers as Jean Sibelius, Arnold Schönberg, and Richard Strauss, and the state of the American novel; and through it all he shows clearly that one America was indeed passing away and that another was being born. And he concludes:

> I wish I could remember where I was when the year came to an end on the night of December 31. Since I had turned thirteen only a week earlier I must have been at home. At 10:30 or thereabouts my father would have been asleep over the *Saturday Evening Post;* my mother, up since 6:30, would have been nodding over her mending. The three young children, a girl and two boys, would have been bedded down for a couple of hours; my older sister was in Dallas, studying music. So I would have gone to the kitchen for a nightly snack: cheese—Herkimer, aged Wisconsin brick, or imported Swiss (none of your devitalized stuff in packages)—or a saucer-full of raw oysters, supplemented with pie and coffee. And then I would have gone to bed, unaware that I had just passed through a pivotal year, and without the slightest suspicion that I would ever write a book about it.

The Automobile

The legislation that came in with the New Freedom undoubtedly paved the way for unending change, and the mass production and labor saving processes devised in places like Detroit did the same; yet it may be that the greatest single instrument of change was the automobile—not the business of making and selling it but the car itself—the bewildering device that gave unlimited freedom of movement and then bound that movement up in a constantly constricting circle, compelling its user to modify almost every aspect of the place where he lives, the place where he works, and his method of getting back and forth between the two.

One would not be much too fanciful to argue that the most momentous problem of the present day is the traffic problem. The trouble with it is that it seems to be basically insoluble, simply because every step taken to reach a solution only makes the problem worse. The automobile has changed both the city and the country, and there are times when it seems to be altogether beyond control; we began by adapting it to our use, and now we are adapting ourselves to its demands. What the end of it all may finally be is beyond human computation.

Some of the aspects of this problem are examined by Mitchell Gordon in an irascible and disturbing book, *Sick Cities: Psychology and Pathology of American Urban Life*. Mr. Gordon holds that our cities are desperately ill, and he feels that the automobile is responsible for much of the illness. He does not profess to see a real cure anywhere, but he does present an arresting study of what the motor car is doing to us—

Sick Cities: Psychology and Pathology of American Urban Life, by Mitchell Gordon. Macmillan Company. 366 pp. $6.50.

of "all the sprawl and congestion that vehicle brings with it wherever it goes."

He argues his case thus: By enabling millions of people to live just about anywhere they choose, instead of remaining close to rapid-transit stations, the automobile has scattered urban populations all over the map. Doing this, it has virtually killed off public transit systems, and it has created a traffic jam of nationwide proportions. More and more cars are hauling fewer and fewer people per trip, and in many cities downtown traffic moves more slowly now than it did in the horse-and-buggy days. When supersonic air transports are in service, it will actually be possible for a traveller to go from Los Angeles to New York more quickly than he can get to and from the airports at each end of the line.

Mr. Gordon presents some figures which are both outlandish and solid.

> The auto's appetite for space is horrendous. The 41,000-mile interstate highway system born with the passage of congressional legislation in 1956 will occupy more land than the entire state of Rhode Island when it is completed in 1972. . . . Two-thirds of Los Angeles' entire downtown area is already given over to the automobile—approximately 33 percent of it to parking lots and garages and the rest to roads and highways. Each one of the city's interchanges, linking one freeway to another, consumes approximately 80 acres of real estate; every mile of freeway, 24. By 1980 the city is expected to have 34 square miles of land devoted to its freeway system—about the size of the entire city of Miami.

The business is expensive—to put a three-mile stretch of freeway through Cleveland it was necessary to remove an estimated $20 million worth of assessed property from the city's tax rolls—and spending money does not seem to help much. In Los Angeles (all of these studies of the dire nature of the traffic problem seem to use that city as the horrible example), Mr. Gordon remarks, $900 million has already been invested in more than 300 miles of freeways and expressways, but municipal highway officials believe that by 1980 they will need more than 1,500 miles of those arteries, for a total investment of more than $5 billion. One official recently remarked that even after all of this is done, traffic conditions by 1980 may well be worse than they are today.

"Statistics tell this poignant tale," says Mr. Gordon. "In the decade from 1947 to 1957, the nation as a whole constructed 53,000 miles of highway lanes while Detroit was stamping out enough automobiles to cover 200,000 miles of highway lanes bumper-to-bumper." He quotes the warning of Urban Land Institute President Boyd Barnard: "The expected increase of automobiles in the next decade will mean bumper-to-bumper traffic not only on all our present roads, turnpikes and expressways, but all those that are in the planning stage as well." Mr. Barnard, apparently, feels that the automobile "has created problems which appear almost insolvable."

Traffic congestion, of course, is not by any means all of the story. The real difficulty, as Mr. Gordon sees it, is what he calls "urban sprawl." The urban area reaches farther and farther into the country, the city decays at its center, problems of schooling, policing, water supply, sanitation, and municipal finance increase more rapidly than they can be handled—and, in short, our cities, where more and more of us live, are being blighted. The author cites the Census Bureau as authority for the statement that more Americans today live in substandard housing than live on farms, and one out of every six dwellings in the nation is either dilapidated or substandard.

Various remedies have been proposed, to be sure—more adequate city planning, comprehensive "urban renewal" programs, and some consolidation of the multiplicity of governmental organization which shares responsibility for such matters. But Mr. Gordon seems to be a pessimist, and he goes on to remark bleakly:

> We can leave our cities pretty much as they are and avoid radical remedies which would drastically remake them. More people in more automobiles, with more time and money to spend keeping them in motion, will speed up the conquest of urban space on earth and, notwithstanding the huge sums that will be poured into new concrete carpeting, compound congestion at critical places. Urban acreage will continue to be ravaged by blight despite vast renewal efforts. Recreational facilities will be harder to reach but more crowded. And, as the sprawling metropolis spreads its jurisdictional patchquilt of governments across the urban landscape, protection from crime, the schooling of underprivileged youth, the disposal of refuse, and a myriad of other local services will be more and more difficult to adequately finance and effectively provide.

Finding a Community

Gloomy enough, all of this, to be sure. Yet the automobile can be blamed too much. The development of the American city has followed its own pattern, and "urban sprawl" had set in well before the requirements of the automobile had had any substantial effect. If urbanization has brought a host of grave problems it appears that it is the city itself, rather than the means men use to get in and out of it and to and fro inside it, that needs examination.

Such an examination, much less emotional and also much more comprehensive and scholarly than the one just cited, is provided in *The Urbanization of America, 1860–1915,* by Blake McKelvey, who undertakes to study what might be called the metropolitan character in America and tries to see just what was going on in the period before the motorcar took over.

In 1860 the Federal Census showed that the United States contained 141 cities, the Census Bureau defining as a city any place that contained more than 8,000 people. Nine of these cities were above the 100,000 mark, and all of them were ports, owing their growth and position largely to water-borne traffic. (They included New York, its sister city Brooklyn, Boston, Philadelphia, Baltimore, New Orleans, St. Louis, Cincinnati, and Chicago.) During the next half century both the number of cities and their respective sizes increased prodigiously; by 1910 there were 228 cities of 25,000 or more, 50 containing more than 100,000, and 8 of more than 500,000.

Clearly enough, the forces that pull men into cities to live and work had been greatly intensified in the years immediately after the Civil War. A big city was no longer of necessity a place based on water transportation; the railroad network was expanding, and the factory town was rising. America was becoming an industrial nation, and there was a new base for metropolitan development. Cities grew faster and larger than ever before, and as they did they tended for a time to become conglomerations of diverse peoples who came surging into centers that were not prepared to handle their social or material needs. It took a long time to bring the evolution of a genuine community out of such conglomerations, and before this happened there were troubles which the muck-rakers discussed as "the shame of the cities" early in this century.

Meanwhile, there were developments. The center of the city became less and less a desirable place to live, and with improved transit facilities people began moving out to the rim; but as they moved out, business people moved in—at least for daytime occupancy—and until around 1920 the trend toward urban concentration continued. Yet all this while, the city was proliferating into suburbs, the center kept thinning out, and presently it was the metropolitan district rather than the city itself that was important.

The city, in short, began to change radically late in the second decade of this century, changing not because of the automobile but because of the nature of its own growth. In effect, it began to turn into something different just as it began to reach maturity; becoming a genuine community, it started to turn into a complex aggregation of communities, with new problems which at bottom are no more difficult than the problems encountered earlier in its growth. The change began before the automobile; as Mr. McKelvey says, the process of urbanization reached its turning point by 1915.

The automobile, in short, is just one problem. There are many problems, all of them arising from the fact that the way we Americans live and work together is undergoing change. As Mr. McKelvey sees it there is no real cause for dismay here. No, the development of the past century has been good. As he sums it up:

> We have seen how policies and techniques of settlement, of production, and of distribution contributed to the growth and decay of cities; how these in turn created civic and social problems that required new adjustments: and how men and women of all ranks and places, organizing to work for the goals they sought, achieved through strife and compromise sufficient economic integration to enable the urban population . . . to attain an unprecedented state of material well-being.

Apparently we have reason to believe that the process will continue.

The Urbanization of America, 1860–1915, by Blake McKelvey. Rutgers University Press. 370 pp. $10.

A TRUE BOSTONIAN

A soul from earth to heaven went.
To whom the saint as he drew near,
Said: "Sir, what claim do you present
To us to be admitted here?"
"In Boston I was born and bred,
And in her schools was educated:
I afterward at Harvard read,
And was with honors graduated.
"In Trinity a pew I own,
Where Brooks is held in such respect,
And the society is known
To be the cream of the select.
"In fair Nahant—a charming spot—
I own a villa, lawns, arcades,
And, last, a handsome burial lot
In dead Mt. Auburn's hallowed shades."
St. Peter mused and shook his head,
Then, as a gentle sigh he drew,
"Go back to Boston, friend," he said,
"Heaven isn't good enough for you."

—The Old Farmer's Almanac